INCLUSIVE
ECONOMIC
THEORY

INCLUSIVE ECONOMIC THEORY

Steven Rosefielde
Ralph W. Pfouts

The University of North Carolina, Chapel Hill, USA

World Scientific

NEW JERSEY · LONDON · SINGAPORE · BEIJING · SHANGHAI · HONG KONG · TAIPEI · CHENNAI

Published by

World Scientific Publishing Co. Pte. Ltd.

5 Toh Tuck Link, Singapore 596224

USA office: 27 Warren Street, Suite 401-402, Hackensack, NJ 07601

UK office: 57 Shelton Street, Covent Garden, London WC2H 9HE

Library of Congress Cataloging-in-Publication Data
Rosefielde, Steven.
   Inclusive economic theory / by Steven Rosefielde, Ralph W. Pfouts.
     pages cm
   Includes bibliographical references.
   ISBN 978-9814566643
   1. Economics--Philosophy. 2. Economics. I. Title.
   HB72.R657 2015
   330.15--dc23

                        2014026650

British Library Cataloguing-in-Publication Data
A catalogue record for this book is available from the British Library.

In-house Editors: Sutha Surenddar/Dong Lixi

Typeset by Stallion Press
Email: enquiries@stallionpress.com

Printed in Singapore

For David Rosefielde

Contents

Acknowledgments

The scope of *Inclusive Economic Theory* is too large to permit us to thank all those who have contributed to its development, but special acknowledgments for their insightful observations are due to Assaf Razin, Stefan Hedlund and Quinn Mills. Teresa Zhou and Wenting Ma provided invaluable research assistance. Susan Rosefielde and June Pfouts gave their unstinting support.

To all, we offer our sincere gratitude.

Steven Rosefielde and R.W. Pfouts

Preface

The goal of *Inclusive Economic Theory* is to tie together various authoritative strands of contemporary economic theory into an easily comprehended whole that illuminates the need for a broader and more realistic approach to contemporary analysis and policymaking undistorted by obsolete 18th century rationalist and 19th century socialist assumptions about utility, ethics, worthiness and traditional culture. This objective was accomplished long ago in other branches of the social sciences and humanities, but the postwar mathematical revolution in economic theory kept economists focused on other concerns.

We attempt to close the gap in economic science by sharply delineating what is knowable and cannot be known about economic motivation, behavior and outcomes at the individual and collective levels, and showing how multiple paradigms can be employed to comprehend prevailing causality in specific cases.

The knowable components of economic motivation, behavior and outcomes at the individual and collective levels involve some aspects of neoclassical microeconomic and macroeconomic theory, entrepreneurship, fundamental determinants of long term economic growth, mathematical correspondences between perfect markets and perfect plans (including regulation), conceptual dimensions of optimal transfers, institutional and policy impacts, linkages between utility and wellbeing (physical and mental health that provide a foundation for fulfillment and contentment) under the influence of ethics, emotions, disturbed psychology, systems and cultures.[1]

We initially believed that our investigation would culminate in a "unified causal field" theory of economics,[2] supposing that Paul Samuelson's method of treating economics primarily as a form of mathematical Newtonian physics,[3] combined with Herbert Simon's and Reinhart Selten's realist refinements,[4] and normative public policy theory might point the

---

[1] Wellbeing is a state of physical, psychological and spiritual health (being well) that allows, but doesn't require people to be fulfilled and content. Utility by contrast is an experience that does't require individuals to be "well." Utility and wellbeing normally should be connected by a function that modifies states of wellbeing for the effect of each new marginal utility experience. Static states of wellbeing are constantly being altered. Utility and wellbeing however aren't always positively correlated because what feels good may not be good for you, judged from the "healthy" perspective assumed by the wellbeing function. Ideally, healthy individuals should take the wellbeing effect of their new marginal choices into account so that utility and wellbeing maximizing come to the same thing, but this is unrealistic. The importance of wellbeing lies in the possibility of improving the incorporation of wellbeing into people's marginal utility choice making. Wellbeing and utility are both "ordinal." Neither can be made cardinal (except in the von Neumann probabilistic sense), nor meaningfully interpersonally added. There is a tendency to conflate wellbeing and happiness. Also, no matter how scholars try to quantify wellbeing external judges are free to independently evaluate outcomes. They are not constrained by the rankings of others. James Griffin (1986), *Well-being*, Oxford: Clarendon Press. Also see Richard Layard, John Helliwell and Jeffrey Sachs, eds., *World Happiness Report 2013* http://unsdsn.org/happiness/. Martin Seligman (2011), *Flourish: A New Understanding of Happiness and Well-being — and How to Achieve Them*, Boston & London: Nicholas Brealey. Nicholas White, N. (2006), *A Brief History of Happiness*, Malden, MA: Blackwell. Cf. Gary Becker (1976), *The Economic Approach to Human Behavior*, Chicago: University of Chicago Press. Gary Becker (1962), "Irrational Behavior and Economic Theory," *Journal of Political Economy*, Vol. 70, No. 1, pp. 1–13.

[2] A unified field theory in physics refers to the possibility of incorporating all fundamental forces and elementary particles in a single field. The term was coined by Albert Einstein who sought to unify the general theory of relativity with electromagnetism. He failed, and no one else has succeeded.

[3] Paul Samuelson (1947). *Foundations of Economic Analysis*, Cambridge: Harvard University Press, 1947. Samuelson was one of the first economists to generalize and apply mathematical methods developed for the study of thermodynamics to economics. His *Foundations of Economic Analysis* is based on the methods of American thermodynamicist Willard Gibbs.

[4] Herbert Simon (1957). "A Behavioral Model of Rational Choice", in Simon, *Models of Man: Social and Rational-Mathematical Essays on Rational Human Behavior in a Social Setting*. New York: Wiley. Herbert Simon (1990), "A Mechanism for Social

way,[5] but were mistaken. It turned out that a "unified field" theory of economics of the kind sought by Albert Einstein in physics is impossible because no plausible set of parsimonious axioms exist that adequately capture the diversity of human behavior.

There isn't one universal explanation of economic behavior. Instead there are three linked complementary paradigms with some shared aspects, each distinguished by its own selective axioms that form an umbrella rather than a unified field theory.

The three paradigms are idealist neoclassical theory, realist neoclassical theory and neo-realism, each subsuming multiple sub-paradigms. The neoclassical paradigms serve admirably when core axioms largely hold, but otherwise they are incomplete and misleading. Neo-realist theory including political economy covers the rest of the territory, but its assumptions are heterogeneous and case specific. The three complementary theories, appropriately linked constitute a framework that offers the prospect of what Karl Popper calls weak knowledge and truthlike verisimilitude.[6]

When the assumptions of ideal neoclassical theory fully apply, they always provide Pareto optimal solutions across space and time. When they don't realist and neo-realist paradigms govern aspects of outcomes, and causalities can be revealed in whole or part by parsing theory and evidence

Selection and Successful Altruism," *Science* 250 (4988), pp. 1665–1668. Herbert Simon (1991). "Bounded Rationality and Organizational Learning," *Organization Science* 2 (1), pp. 125–134. Gerd Gigerenzer, and Reinhard Selten (2002), *Bounded Rationality*. Cambridge: MIT Press. Ariel Rubinstein (1998), *Modeling Bounded Rationality*. MIT Press. Clem Tisdell, Clem (1996). *Bounded Rationality and Economic Evolution: A Contribution to Decision Making, Economics, and Management*, Cheltenham, UK: Brookfield, 1998. Daniel Kahneman (2003), "Maps of Bounded Rationality: Psychology for Behavioral Economics," *The American Economic Review* 93 (5), 2003, pp. 1449–1475.
[5]See Abram Bergson (1976), "Social Choice and Welfare Economics under Representative Government," *Journal of Economics*, 6(3) (October), 1976, pp. 171–190.
[6]Karl Popper (1973), *Conjectures and Refutations: The Growth of Scientific Knowledge*, London: Routledge; Popper, 'A Note on Verisimilitude', *The British Journal for the Philosophy of Science*, 27 (1976): 147–159. Karl Popper (1962), *The Open Society and Its Enemies*, New York: Harper & Row. Popper (1985), "The Rationality Principle," in: David Miller (ed.) *Popper Selections*, Princeton: Princeton University Press.

with critical rationality to identify truthlike verisimilitudes, "truths" that can evaluated further with Bergsonian welfare theory.[7]

Inclusive economic theory consequently provides richer insight into causality than neoclassical theory, and affords the prospect of superior public policy making, even though it cannot resolve all disputes and paradoxes.

---

[7]Abram Bergson (1938), "A Reformulation of Certain Aspects of Welfare Economics," *Quarterly Journal of Economics*, 52, 1, pp. 210–234.

About the Authors

 Steven Rosefielde received an AM degree in Soviet Regional Studies (1967) and Ph.D. in Economics from Harvard University (1972). His special areas were Soviet economy and comparative systems theory including Asian economic systems, labor managed firms and international trade. He was trained by Abram Bergson, working as well with Wassily Leontief, Alexander Gerschenkron, Simon Kuznets, Gottfried von Haberler and Evsei Domar. He is a Professor of Economics at the University of North Carolina, and has served simultaneously as Adjunct Professor at various universities including the U.S. Naval Postgraduate School, Monterey. He has taught widely across the globe in Russia, Japan, China, and Thailand, and has been a visiting research scholar at the Stockholm School of Economics, Bank of Finland, Trento University, Central Economics and Mathematics Institute (Moscow). During the Soviet era, he was an advisor to the Office of the American Secretary of Defense and FOI (Swedish Defense Institute), also serving as Coordinator of the US–USSR Joint Cooperative Research Program on Science and Technology (between the National Science Foundation and the Soviet Academy of Sciences), Topic 1, Subtopic 3, "Enterprise modeling," 1977–1981. In 1997, he was inducted into the Russian Academy of Natural Sciences [Rossiiskaia Akademiia Estestvennykh Nauk (RAEN)]. After the Soviet Union collapsed, he refocused his attention on Asia and the European Union while remaining actively engaged with Russia and Eastern

Europe. Throughout his career he has striven to integrate the lessons learned in high-level government service with advanced economic theory.

 Ralph William Pfouts was born on September 9, 1920. He graduated Phi Beta Kappa from the University of Kansas in 1942 before joining the navy. He received his M.A. in 1947 and Ph.D. in economics from the University of North Carolina in 1952. He and Kenneth Arrow were Harold Hotelling's most famous students. He taught at the University of North Carolina from 1952 until his retirement in 1987, serving as Chairman of the Economics Department 1962–1968. He was both vice president and president of the Southern Economic Association (1961–1962; 1965–1966) as well as the Atlantic Economic Society (1973–1976; 1977–1978), which bestowed a Lifetime Achievement Award on him in 2008. He also held responsible positions in the American Economic Association, the American Statistical Association, and the Econometric Society. He was a visiting scholar at the Massachusetts Institute of Technology (1962–1963) where he worked closely with Paul Samuelson on consumption theory and the theory of multiproduct firms. His research was concentrated in mathematical microeconomics and statistics. In his later years his research focused on satisficing theory and fuzzy sets; an effort that culminated in the *magnum opus* R.W. Pfouts and Steven Rosefielde, *Inclusive Economic Theory*, Singapore: World Scientific Publishers, 2014.

Introduction

Inclusive Economic Theory is designed to probe the limits of the neo-classical paradigm broadly construed as a technique for drawing valid "positive" and "normative" inferences about real economic behavior, with an eye toward overcoming deficiencies by providing inclusive guidance on how to impartially proceed when neoclassical theorems fail to correspond with observed behavior.[1] The project is more ambitious than

---

[1]Rosenberg and Curtain deny that economics can ever become a science, but they draw their inferences one-sidedly from the neoclassical experience. See Alex Rosenberg and Tyler Curtain, "What is Economics Good For?" *The Stone*, August 24, 2013. They then go on to contradict themselves about the indeterminism of neoclassical economics by claiming that it can be employed as it stands as an indispensable tool for government and social activism. "So if predictive power is not in the cards for economics, what is it good for? Social and political philosophers have helped us answer this question, and so understand what economics is really all about. Since Hobbes, philosophers have been concerned about the design and management of institutions that will protect us from "the knave" within us all, those parts of our selves tempted to opportunism, free riding and generally avoiding the costs of civil life while securing its benefits. Hobbes and, later, Hume — along with modern philosophers like John Rawls and Robert Nozick — recognized that an economic approach had much to contribute to the design and creative management of such institutions. Fixing bad economic and political institutions (concentrations of power, collusions and monopolies), improving good ones (like the Fed's open-market operations), designing new ones (like electromagnetic bandwidth auctions), in the private and public sectors, are all attainable tasks of economic theory." *Inclusive Economic Theory* rejects this backhanded neoclassical optimism. Progress is possible, but requires the full development of neo-realist theory and practice. Inclusive economic theory moreover is nonpartisan, and doesn't service as a clarion call for populist social democratic activism.

1

simply elevating the status of social concerns in contemporary economic policymaking.[2]

Faith in the cogency of neoclassical premises, the theory's logical consistency, comprehensiveness, predictive power and normative merit runs very deep among economists (but not political scientists, anthropologists and sociologists) making it difficult for many economists to believe that individuals, groups, authorities and policymakers from time to time significantly and persistently deviate from the neoclassical script and/or "misbehave."[3] They are inclined to believe that political economy, anthropological economy and sociological economy are secondary normative matters that properly should take a back seat to competitive individual utility optimizing and are best dealt with through democratically approved minority protections.

Neoclassical economists are predisposed to surmise that what ought to be is actually what transpires.[4] Or, if people don't act according to the axioms of competitive rational choice, they ought to, and should be coached whenever they fail to grasp the rationalist imperative. It is easy to sympathize with the presumption. Few people admit that they lack complete, well-formed preferences; that they erratically shop and choose impulsively. Few people acknowledge that they are sometimes unscrupulous. Authorities

---

[2]The term inclusive economics is used by other authors to mean different things. The OECD uses it as concept supporting the claim that NGOs and other local organizations enhance market performance. See *The Social Economy: Building Inclusive Economies*, http://www.oecd.org/regional/leed/thesocialeconomybuildinginclusiveeconomies.htm. The nascent inclusive economics literature is very soft, consisting mostly of admonitions to integrate ethics into neoclassical theory, and embrace the concept of wellbeing in lieu of utility, without adding anything substantial to the established body of normative theory. There have been no attempts to construct a fully integrated body of neo-realist economic theory of the sort developed in this treatise. See http://www.stwr.org/economic-sharing-alternatives/when-growth-is-empty-towards-an-inclusive-economics.html Ganesh Rauniyar and Ravi Kanbur, "Inclusive Development: Two Papers on Conceptualization, Application and the ADB Perspective," *Journal of the Asia Pacific Economy*, Vol. 15, No. 4, 2010, pp. 437–469.

[3]There are many exceptions. For example, see Stephen Marglin, *The Dismal Science: How Thinking like an Economists Undermines Community*, Cambridge MA: Harvard University Press, 2008. Amartya Sen, *The Idea of Justice*, London: Penguin, 2010. Joseph Stiglitz, *Globalization and its Discontents*, London: Penguin, 2002.

[4]Voltaire, *Candide, ou l'Optimisme*, 1759.

never admit that they subordinate the people's interests to their own private advantage.

It will be shown that while neoclassical theory is indispensable in many circumstances, inferences drawn from its axioms are often seriously misleading on matters of fundamental importance.

Investigative Structure

The inclusive economic theory elaborated in this treatise unfolds in three steps. Part I tells the neoclassical story. It traces its idealist intellectual roots and probes the nuances of the competitive ideal. It also recapitulates neoclassical idealism's bounded rational vulnerabilities, and lays out the requirements for realistic alternatives from soup to nuts; that is, from consumer behavior to democratic public programming. Part II relaxes conventional Enlightenment assumptions about the power of reason and mankind's moral perfectibility and then elaborates a range of neo-realist alternatives. Part III links complementary idealist, realist and neo-realist economic paradigms under an inclusive umbrella that allows analysts to identify "truth" using Karl Popper's concepts of critical rationality and truth-like verisimilitude.

Part I

Neoclassical Economics

Chapter 1

Rational Utilitarianism

Economics Before the Age of Reason

The first treatise on economics before the Age of Reason, once ascribed to Aristotle (384–322 BC), is now attributed to one of his successors. It was written in three short volumes, only two of which survive in the original Greek. *Oeconomicus* (οἰκονομία) elaborates the principles of gentlemanly farming and is a manual on good household administration. The others provide examples and extensions, but neither explores markets nor political economy. The post-Aristotelean literature likewise addressed special topics instead of universal principles connecting production, consumption, distribution, transfer and finance throughout the Roman period and the Middle-Ages. There were no systematic, integrated scientific treatises or theories which today constitute the "neoclassical" core.

Foundations of Modern Economic Theory
in the Age of Reason

The hypothesis that the independent endeavors of "household managers" with disparate skills and abilities promote the wealth of nations eluded political and social thinkers for 2000 years after Aristotle. It first surfaced in the Enlightenment (1650–1790), often described as the Age of Reason. The period is bounded by the works of Baruch Spinoza (1632–1677) and John Locke (1632–1704) at one end of the spectrum, and the French Revolution (1789) at the other. The Enlightenment coincided with the Age of Absolutism and was superseded in the 19th century by Romanticism.

The goal of Enlightenment thinkers, which required the entire tool box of the neoclassical core, was to create a design for living that allowed everyone to achieve superior states of wellbeing (utility) by choosing rationally, free from the counterclaims of state, community, family and religious authority. The Philosophes asserted that individuals regardless of rank, gender, race, ethnicity or religion were autonomous, and in this sense were born equal, but found themselves everywhere in chains.[1] Authority unjustly deprived them of the right to choose in their mundane pursuits, and more subtly the right to seek personal fulfillment. Authority had to be overthrown and mankind liberated.[2]

The validity of this concept of autonomy, equality, freedom, fulfillment and justice was attributed to "reason," understood as a set of logically consistent idealist axioms and constructs. Enlightenment thinkers were able to show to their own satisfaction that if their "plausible" assumptions were accepted and applied, then the results would be beneficial.

Most of these axioms (the virtues of equality, freedom, etc.) were normative and could be easily challenged on philosophical grounds,[3] but one was behavioral and involved reason in a different sense. Enlightenment thinkers, following Socrates,[4] claimed that all humans possessed intellect; that every individual had the capacity to analyze, evaluate and choose based on ethical imperatives and a multitude of perceptive, cognitive, conceptual, emotional, spiritual, and physical factors. Individuals consequently were not only free to choose, but more importantly everyone was able to make the right choices by using reason to thoroughly appraise and select best options. People didn't need authority because they could act rationally on their own behalf.

---

[1] Jean-Jacques Rousseau (1754). *Discourse on the Origin and Basis of Inequality Among Men* (*Discours sur l'origine et les fondements de l'inégalité parmi les hommes*).

[2] Many Philosophes like Thomas Hobbes and even Rousseau himself considered people to be corrupt. Those among them championing democracy and *laissez-faire* disposed of the claim that the people were too immoral to rule, by contending that reason provided a mechanism enabling men to overcome their viciousness.

[3] Plato (1994). *Republic*, trans. Robin Waterfield, Oxford: Oxford University Press.

[4] Plato demonstrates in the Meno that a slave is capable of learning a geometrical truth because "he already has the knowledge in his soul." The slave is able to "reason." See *Plato in Twelve Volumes*, Vol. 3 translated by W. R. M. Lamb, Cambridge, MA, Harvard University Press, 1967.

The same principle was said to hold in people's public pursuits. Enlightenment thinkers contended that every person should be able to participate in governing on an equal footing within families, communities and states because reason empowered them to do so, and any other form of authority was rejected as oppressive. This made democracy (people's rule) the only legitimate form of government. The people themselves must govern public life, just as their private existences, a concept that eventually became the touchstone of contemporary notions of democratic free enterprise.[5]

Sin and Practical Reason

The rationalist manifesto was vulnerable to a wide array of religious critiques from the broadly accepted Christian doctrine of Original Sin to the Calvinist premise that mankind was "totally corrupt."[6] The Enlightenment claim that rationality provided a stout defense against corruption appeared absurd to pious Christians, undermining the credibility of Spinoza's, Locke's and Rousseau's (1712–1778) revolutionary program. If bad people liberated themselves from authority devout Christians expected evil consequences.

The Right Thing to Do

A solution to this conundrum was proposed by Immanuel Kant (1724–1804) in a series of treatises published between 1785 and 1797.[7] He identified a class of widely accepted moral laws called "categorical imperatives" founded on reason like the Christian golden rule: "Do unto others as you would wish others to do unto you."[8] Kant argued that these moral laws allow individuals to operate autonomously in beneficent ways without external

---

[5]Joseph Schumpeter (2010). *Capitalism, Socialism and Democracy*, 2nd ed., New York: Martino Fine Books; Arrow, Kenneth (1963). *Social Choice and Individual Values*, 2nd ed., New York: Wiley.

[6]The doctrine of Original Sin is not found in Judaism.

[7]*Groundwork of the Metaphysic of Morals* (1785), *Critique of Practical Reason* (1788), and *Metaphysics of Morals (1797)*. Cf. Michael Sandel (2010). *Justice: What is the Right Thing to Do?* New York: Macmillan.

[8]Matthew 7:12.

authority solely on the basis of reason, and conjectured that people would feel morally obligated to do so.

Kant's construct provided much needed support for Spinoza's, Locke's and Rousseau's claim that human liberation and democracy would yield positive results, despite mankind's alleged "total depravity." It didn't prove that individuals would behave as reason taught they ought, but the categorical imperative did create a presumption that they might. If people convinced themselves that behaving righteously was the "right thing to do," then liberation and democracy might be blessings. Achieving a virtuous outcome wouldn't be easy. Philosophers would have to create a set of Kantian moral laws to cover most contingencies, and ordinary people would have to master their rational obligations, but the undertaking no longer could be dismissed as fatuous.

Self-Interest and the Invisible Hand

Kant's moral imperative despite its rational appeal was effectively dead on arrival as a scientific explanation of human behavior because few could master its requirements, and fewer tried. Perhaps, mankind could do the right thing, but it wouldn't if everyone had to be an accomplished Kantian moral philosopher.

A more convincing solution to the paradox of personal freedom and democracy was needed and it was provided by Adam Smith (1723–1790) who had the wit to see that humanity was only partially corrupt, and that the evil men wish to do can be greatly mitigated by competition in business, private affairs and government. Smith applauded righteous self-discipline in his *The Theory of Moral Sentiments* (1759), but realized that people could improve their own wellbeing and others even when operating with mixed motives.

The mixed motive that impressed Smith was the desire to better oneself by exploiting (1) opportunities and (2) people. The first motive he showed was constructive. People seek the best education and training, the best employment, and strive to use their resources wisely. Proprietors, manufacturers, and merchants endeavor to satisfy customers and maximize profits. Elected officials have an interest in pleasing voters. Spinoza's, Locke's and Rousseau's advocacy of liberation and democracy on these scores was likely to be more beneficial than they themselves may have understood precisely because the rational pursuit of self-betterment enabled people to realize part of their untapped potential.

Smith conceded that individuals often had ulterior motives; that they were inclined to advance their personal interests at the expense of others, raising the possibility that their evil doings might outweigh the good. But he observed that the problem could be mitigated by establishing proper institutions, including Locke's social contract, Roman rule of law, and unfettered competition. Yes, there was Original Sin, but this didn't invalidate the Enlightenment case for liberation and democracy. All the good things that Spinoza, Locke, Rousseau and Kant promised could be achieved by combining people's rational desire for self-betterment with the "invisible hand."

Utilitarianism

Smith's insight that people competitively pursue their self-interest struck his supporters on reflection as self-evident, but concealed an important perplexity. How did people go about evaluating their self-betterment? How did they commensurate the comparative worth of coffee and tea?

Jeremy Bentham (1748–1832) proposed a hedonistic solution in his *The Principles of Morals and Legislation* (written in 1780) where he argued first that people desired things that gave them utility (enhanced happiness or reduced suffering),[9] and second that "utilities" could be ordered, ranked, quantified, added and multiplied across individuals.[10] These claims meant that the human mind reduces "expected" sensations to a common denominator that allows individuals to choose rationally and consistently. Smith as Bentham saw the matter not only was right that people could beneficially pursue their self-interest, but he contended they could do so with precision, and compute aggregate societal happiness too.

Bentham's claims led economists in two disparate directions. The possibility of a precise utilitarian calculus fostered a marginalist revolution

---

[9]Hedonistic utilitarianism is a special case of "consequentialism," and can be refined to include aspects of virtue ethics. See Portmore, Douglas (2011). *Commonsense Consequentialism: Wherein Morality Meets Rationality*, New York: Oxford University Press.

[10]Bentham's utilitarianism had antecedents. Many eighteenth-century Italian mercantilists including Antonio Genovesi, and Marchese Cesare di Beccaria held that value was explained in terms of the general utility and scarcity of things.

that enabled analysts to comprehensively investigate human choice on the supposition that Bentham was correct, at least with respect to ordinality. This advanced the Enlightenment project.

Bentham's belief in the cardinal additivity of interpersonal utility (a more demanding assumption than ordinality),[11] however went further. It created a metric that could be used to evaluate the collective merit of individual self-seeking. Where Smith, Spinoza, Locke, and Rousseau thought that liberation was enough (that there was no need for cardinal additivity), Bentham's human happiness calculus implied that an objective case could be made for subordinating individuals to moral and social authority (the greatest happiness of the greatest number is the measure of right and wrong).[12] Where Kant had sought to create a virtuous society by preaching the gospel of personal duty, Bentham strove to create the foundation for morally principled state regulation and transfers on a cardinal utilitarian basis for society's hedonistic betterment. Societies that maximized collective utility, as distinct from each individual maximizing his or her utility were best. Benthamite "social" (collective) democracy on this score trumped democratic free enterprise.[13]

Marginalist Revolution

The power of Bentham's utilitarianism didn't lie in its objective validity,[14] but came from its analytic fruitfulness. While the physics, psychology

---

[11] Ordinal utility functions are unique up to positive monotone transformations, while cardinal utility functions are unique up to positive linear transformations. An additive dimension to individual ordinal calculus can be achieved by offering individuals choices where the likelihood of acquisition depends on assigned probabilities. This permits individuals not only to order their preferences, but to quantify them additively in specific contexts, and illuminates how people could try to precisely weigh their alternatives. The tactic cannot be extended to assessing collective interpersonal expected utility. See John von Neumann and Oskar Morgenstern, Oskar (1944). *Theory of Games and Economic Behavior*. Princeton, NJ: Princeton University Press.

[12] Jeremy Bentham (1776). *A fragment on Government*, London Preface (paragraph 2).

[13] Cf. Yuval Levin (2013). *The Great Debate: Edmund Burke, Thomas Paine, and the Birth of Right and Left*, New York: Basic Books, 2013.

[14] People can distinguish pleasure and pain, but they also can modify these sensations by mental discipline. Furthermore, pleasure and pain are ambiguously connected with merit and virtue. There is no strictly positive correlation between pleasure and beneficial behavior,

and meaning of expected utility still remain obscure, the concept allowed William Stanley Jevons (1835–1882),[15] Carl Menger (1840–1921),[16] and Marie-Esprit-Leon Walras (1834–1910) to elaborate how incremental choices are made by individuals operating interactively in markets.[17] Their approach remains the cornerstone of contemporary neoclassical economic theory in Adam Smith's Enlightenment tradition stressing the explanatory power of self-interest and competition whether or not people are fundamentally moral or utility is cardinally additive.[18]

Marginal ordinal utility theory is compatible with Bentham's assumption that individual utilitarian experiences (but not collective) can cumulate into better and better states of wellbeing, if and only if physically and mentally healthy people always choose wisely. Otherwise, marginalism merely illuminates momentary intent without connecting a sequence of independent experiences with rationally constructed psychological states.

Beyond the Enlightenment Project

The Enlightenment faith in the power of reason to beneficently liberate humanity from all authoritarian oppression explains why economists remain broadly content with marginalism despite a welter of mixed evidence.[19] Theoreticians advocate competitive markets in a world where individuals in a strict sense seldom utility optimize and big business, big social advocacy and big government sometimes collusively craft national

---

although the link would be stronger if people could foresee the full consequences of their actions and adjust their hedonistic calculus accordingly.

[15] William Stanley Jevons, "A General Mathematical Theory of Political Economy," 1863, and *The Theory of Political Economy*, 1871.

[16] *Grundsätze der Volkswirtschaftslehre*, 1871.

[17] Marie-Esprit-Leon Walras (1874). *Éléments d'économie politique pure*.

[18] Arrow, Kenneth J. (1987). "Rationality of Self and Others in An Economic System," in R. M. Hogarth and M. W. Reder (eds.), *Rational Choice*. Chicago: The University of Chicago Press.

[19] On the plus side, living standards have improved under democratic rule. On the negative side of the ledger, democracies are beset with inequities and injustices, while authoritarianism persists and sometimes performs in a superior manner.

economic policies to further their interests at the people's expense,[20] because they are predisposed by a faith in rationality to believe that the invisible hand is more or less effective. Like many of their brethren in other social sciences and the humanities, they still worship in the "temple of reason."[21]

Some perhaps also believe that political programs and transfers are broadly guided by Benthamite hedonistic collective utility maximizing. Unfortunately, they are too hopeful. Real behavior and policies deviate diversely from the rational competitive utility maximizing ideal among other reasons because some individuals succeed in exerting power that benefits the few at the expense of the many. This occurs at multiple levels including families, communities and nations. Individual utility maximizing and optimizing also are incomplete. People satisfice by incompletely utility searching compared with the competitive ideal due to psychological flaws of various types, deference, acquiescence, compulsion and lack of concentration. Individuals fail to utility maximize, optimize and satisfice because they are perplexed and don't understand what they should be maximizing. Individuals are overwhelmed by contradictory information and don't know how to efficiently cope. Individuals are disconcerted by uncertainty, paradox and mood changes. Many individuals are neurotic, psychotic and subject to addictions that prevent them from maximizing, optimizing and satisficing. Individuals are deceived by other individuals, groups, authorities and the state. Individuals frequently don't learn adequately from repeated personal, familial, community and governmental failure. Individuals are unable to make complex net benefit calculations. Families, communities and governments don't maximize the collective interest as claimed.

Moreover, all utility doesn't derive from competitive search. People may benefit or suffer (utility/disutility) from obligations imposed on

---

[20] Steven Rosefielde and Daniel Quinn Mills (2013). *Democracy and Its Elected Enemies: American Political Capture and Economic Decline*, Cambridge: Cambridge University Press.

[21] The French Revolution was interpreted by its leaders as the triumph of reason over religion, prompting a "cult of reason" and the temporary conversion of churches like Paris's Notre Dame into "temples of reason".

them, that is, from what Martin Heidegger calls "being in the world" (serendipitous experiences). They may feel pleasure and pain from instinctually, emotionally and intuitively driven activities, or even illusory experiences (daydreams, misunderstanding, and delusions). Authorities claim to act in the collective interest, but pursue their private interests instead. Authorities don't know how to maximize their private interests.

These "disturbances" have normative and positive implications. First and foremost, they tell us that Enlightenment faith in the beneficence and curative powers of reason and by extension the neoclassical core is overdrawn. Second, they reveal that valid judgments about the rationality of outcomes cannot be deduced without ascertaining how decisions are actually made. Third, competition cannot overcome the opportunities missed due to faulty psychological calculation and decision making. Fourth, imperfectly competitive individualist systems aren't necessarily second best when proper account is taken of their persistence and how individuals really calculate utility and choose. Satisficing strategies (judged from the standpoint of the competitive ideal) may be better than imperfectly competitive ones (where the powerful optimize in their own interest). Fifth, families, communities and governments are almost never the beneficent units they pretend to be, complicating the assessment of economic welfare potential. Sixth, the competitive neoclassical concept of economic utility is incomplete. It omits many essential utilitarian experiences. Seventh, the concept of competitive market utilitarianism taken on faith is misleading because it deflects attention from the shortcomings of real outcomes. National economic performance is better assessed with composite measures of wellness (physical and mental health), consciousness, economic justice, personal fulfillment and contentment.[22]

Beyond Idealism

The Enlightenment dream in various guises ranging from democratic free enterprise to democratic socialism (Benthamite collectivist variant) has

---

[22]This is the position of "virtue ethics." For example see Deidre McCloskey (2007). *The Bourgeois Virtues: Ethics for an Age of Commerce*, Chicago: University of Chicago Press.

its charms, but is an inadequate scientific substitute for inclusive welfare improving systems. It must be supplemented with accurate assessments of how and why people and policymakers actually behave in diverse circumstances to gauge how outcomes deviate from "rational" competitive potential and how they can be best improved.

Chapter 2

Competitive Ideal

Neoclassical Idealism

Contemporary economic theories of most varieties are founded on the premise that reason guides peoples' utility-seeking. Rational idealists, in the spirit of Enlightenment Philosophes claim that reason and competition are sufficient to assure ideal outcomes as individuals self-perceive them,[1] subject to various minor qualifications. Satisficers (Herbert Simon) paint a more objective picture, and neo-realists investigate economic possibilities suggested by other concepts and mechanisms.[2]

This chapter succinctly elaborates the essentials of idealist neoclassical theory as a benchmark for discussing realist refinements and supplementary neo-realist constructs. It emphasizes the basics, disregarding profound axiomatic defects that will be thoroughly examined later in Chapters 4 and 5.

Rational Economy

Neoclassical economic theory teaches that every individual can actualize his or her full human potential within certain natural limits under the rule of law, through market competition in the private sector and democratic governance

---

[1] Jean-Jacques Rousseau contended that if people were permitted to act solely on reason, the paradox that "Man is born free and everywhere is in chains" would be happily resolved. Rousseau (1762). *The Social Contract, Book I,* Chapter 1.

[2] "Man does not live by bread alone." *bible.cc/matthew/4-4.htm* Neo-realists don't confine themselves to the rational individualist, utilitarian, ethically and community neutral models of ideal organization and social control. See Chapter 10.

in the public domain. The competitive and democratic assumptions exclude the possibility of sustained monopolistic distortions and insider governance, although this condition can be softened for the short run by invoking the concept of workable competition.[3] All individuals in the perfectly competitive paradigm are assumed to have equal political, civil, and business opportunity. They advance their wellbeing by utility seeking in the private sector, and avail themselves of democratic government services whenever the state is a least cost provider. The primary functions of democratic government are providing public services, administering the law, and regulating the economy as the majority desires, subject to various constitutional protections.

The characteristics of the neoclassical ideal can be best illustrated in the factor, production, distribution and income transfer spaces with standard geometry, assuming that utility seekers offer their labor to the point

---

[3]The term workable competition implies a high, but imperfect degree of competition. Systems that are less than workably competitive can be described as anticompetitive. The concept covers both the private and public sectors. Steven Rosefielde and Daniel Quinn Mills (2013). *Democracy and Its Elected Enemies: American Political Capture and Decline*, Cambridge: Cambridge University Press. Rulers craft economic systems to serve their purposes, constrained by culture and established institutions. They adorn their actions with noble concepts like free enterprise, democratic socialism, communism and ummah to garner support, without unduly constraining themselves. All systems regardless of ideology are compatible with a wide range of policies across the political spectrum from radical to ultra conservative, as long as fundamentals aren't infringed. Communist societies, whether market or planned, must suppress non-communist influences in pursuing party objectives. The corporatist organization of European Union societies can be employed for progressive or Nazi purposes. American free enterprise has accommodated both slavery and minority empowerment without violating its constitution.

As a consequence, although politics everywhere is important, culture and institutions play a more enduring role in determining how systems are organized. Even in extreme cases where communists have seized power and criminalized the market, prior regimes always have been autocratic and undeveloped with feeble market penetration. Communist ideology was less potent in determining the choice of directive methods than commonly supposed.

Culture as employed in this text, therefore, always means the written and unwritten rules that govern individual and collective utility seeking. If society is acculturated to providing equal opportunity, then politics will be correspondingly restrained. However, in most instances entrenched patterns of privilege and deference, codified formally and informally in institutions empower some at the expense of others. The patterns of privilege, including the mechanisms of enforcement determine each system's signature.

where the value of leisure and additional work at the margin are equal, and employers hire workers until the value of their marginal products equal the competitive wage. Employers profit maximize, given competitively determined product prices, and employees utility maximize, earning incomes and enjoying leisure given equilibrium wages. As a consequence, consumers are sovereign; that is, the supplies produced competitively maximize their utility.

Most consumer goods are bought in retail outlets, where once again profit maximizing and utility maximizing govern product distribution to final buyers. If people are uncharitable, this constitutes the social welfare maximum otherwise, the analysis proceeds to the goods transfer space, where each individual decides how much of his or her income should be bestowed upon others.

Each phase of the competitive maximization process in the private sector is governed by a logic known as Pareto optimality,[4] where transactions continue until it is impossible to voluntarily improve one person's utility without diminishing the utility of another. The composite maximization is often described as Pareto ideal, or a Pareto general equilibrium, and applies to all business and civic activities. Public programs operate according to similar principles, but differ in important details because balloting provides officials with less information about people's preferences than direct face-to-face discussion and negotiation.

Pareto Efficiency

These concepts can be expressed graphically with the aid of analytic geometry. There are four spaces that require close consideration: factor, production, distribution, and welfare.

Factor supply and allocation in the private sector are connected with production in the Edgeworth–Bowley box displayed in Figure 2.1. The coordinate axes forming the sides of the box indicate voluntary equilibrium supplies of capital (k) and labor (l). The sides end where the derived utility in consumption of each factor is just equal to the foregone value of leisure. Their dimensions can change with the credit supply and workers' attitudes

---

[4]Vilfredo Pareto (1906). *Manuel of Political Economy.*

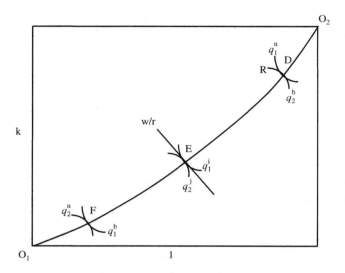

Figure 2.1   Pareto Factor Allocation.

toward leisure. Tightened credit and increased leisure reduce GDP, but this will be optimal if it maximizes utility even though it might superficially seem like a depression.

The box's interior contains all possible allocations of labor and capital in the production of the two goods (q_1) and (q_2) shown at the lower and upper intersection of coordinate axes (their origins). The space also contains two nested, convex, radial sets of isoquants (production functions: $q = F(k, l)$), one for each good. These are the best technologies in the sense that they max- imize profits and individual utilities. The value of the superscripts on every isoquant, is the highest competitively attainable. The further any isoquant lies from its respective origin, the higher the output level designated by the isoquant superscripts.

If an economy is in a state of total utility maximizing equilibrium, there must be one corresponding point inside the Edgeworth–Bowley box. This point represents the utility optimizing supply assortment, and the maximum volumes consistent with it. If they didn't, the utility maximizing process would be incomplete. The condition can be geometrically expressed as an isoquant double tangency (point E) because production at other points along either isoquant would mean that more of q_1 or q_2 could be generated without lowering the output of the other, again implying that optimization was incomplete. The price line at all double tangencies is the wage–rental ratio. The only factual equilibrium is at point E.

It is also possible to imagine a set of Pareto equilibria for alternative configurations of factor and product demand (caused by a change of individuals' taste). These entail minor adjustments of the sides of the Edgeworth–Bowley box (not shown), and correspond with other isoquant double tangencies. The set of all efficient factor supply, input allocation, and production points, actual or counterfactual is called the contract curve, and represents a menu of actual and potential Pareto optimal outputs (GDPs). The locus is useful because it allows us to visualize the characteristics of inferior economies. Any point other than E along the contract curve like D or F, is inferior because the goods supplied don't maximize open society consumer utility. The outputs at D and F could be efficiently produced, if demand were different but it isn't. And of course, if the economy operated at point R, off the contract curve, it would be even more inferior because factor miss allocation means that society could have done better by sliding down the isoquant to point D, increasing the production of one good, while holding the supply of the other fixed. All counterfactual outcomes on the contract curve are classified as technically efficient because even though consumers dislike them, they could be counterfactually ideal. All other points in the Edgeworth–Bowley box are technically and economically inefficient because they fail to maximize utility and minimize system wide cost. E and only E is the true Pareto equilibrium.

These principles are depicted in an alternative way in the private sector production space (Figure 2.2). The coordinate axes represent outputs q_1 and q_2 instead of the factors k and l, which have been suppressed. The space inside the coordinate axes contains the equilibrium production point E, and all counterfactual Pareto equilibria like D and F forming the contract curve in Figure 2.1. This locus remapped in the production space is called the production possibility frontier (PPF), and like its Edgeworth–Bowley box twin serves as a Paretian supply ideal for two products jointly. As before, point E and only point E is a true Paretian equilibrium. Other points on the PPF are technically, but not economically efficient, and all points off the frontier are inefficient, although it can be said that points along the ray from the origin through E other than E, are right assortments in the wrong volumes, and economically efficient in an technically inferior sense.

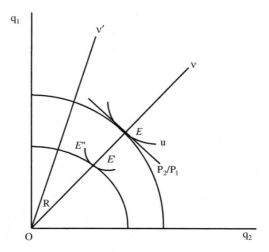

Figure 2.2   Pareto Efficiency Possibilities.

The merit of any nation's economic performance is easily evaluated with this conceptual apparatus. Insofar, as incomplete profit-seeking and authoritarian public programs supersede consumer and popular preferences, a country cannot operate at the Pareto ideal point E. Nor can it be technically efficient with respect to counterfactual individual demand for the same reasons. It necessarily operates below (E' or E''), on a rent-granting constrained production feasibility frontier (PFF), due to the intrinsic deficiencies of its imperfectly competitive authoritarianism.

Distributional merit can also be illustrated geometrically with reference to the Pareto standard. The Edgeworth–Bowley box employed for this purpose, and displayed in Figure 2.3 takes the equilibrium private sector outputs q_1 and q_2, (points E in Figures 2.1 and 2.2), and arrays them unit by unit along the coordinate axes without regard to how they are distributed to income earning claimants A and B. The end points represent the total amount of each good available for distribution between individuals A and B in a two-participant economy. Points at the southwest and northeast vertices, and in the box's interior represent feasible distributions of the goods between the parties, who are guided by their convex, nested ordinal indifference curves (iso-utility) radiating from the lower and upper origins.

$$[U_A = G(q_1, q_2); \ U_B = H(q_1, q_2)].$$

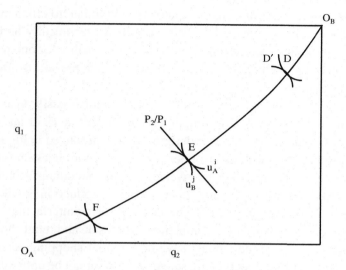

Figure 2.3   Pareto Retail Distribution.

If an economy is in a state of total utility maximizing equilibrium, there must be one corresponding corner or inside point in the Edgeworth–Bowley distribution space. This point represents the utility optimizing retail allocation of the Pareto ideal output supply because, otherwise, the utility maximizing process would be incomplete. It is achieved through unfettered negotiation, given the wages and rents earned by claimants A and B in Figure 2.1. The condition is expressed geometrically as an indifference curve double tangency (point E) because distribution at any other point along either iso-utility curve would mean that one participant could attain greater utility without reducing the other's utility, given the equilibrium income distribution. The price line P_2/P_1 at the double tangency E is the only true price equilibrium.

Point E is the only Pareto efficient distribution in the Edgeworth–Bowley box, but if tastes were different (given the same retail supplies), or there were post-production tax-transfers altering the distribution of purchasing power, a locus of counterfactual Pareto ideal distributions would be generated, represented by the contract curve in Figure 2.3. Just as in the production case, contract curve points other than E can be viewed as technically efficient in the sense that the distribution would be ideal, if purchasing power were allocated in some alternative Pareto efficient way. Points off the contract curve, however, are always technically and economically inefficient because better outcomes are possible for one participant without reducing the utility of the other, given the prevailing after-tax income distribution.

The distributional inefficiency of any retail sector is easily visualized with the aid of Figure 2.3. Consumption cannot occur at E, or any other point on the contract curve if the underlying supply produced in Figure 2.2 lies on a production feasibility frontier because, technologies chosen are inferior, or factors are misallocated given the factual or counterfactual state of demand. And, even if the country operates on its production possibilities frontier, retail distribution can only be factually or counterfactually efficient if there were no barriers to competitive wholesale and retail shopping access. Wherever some individuals have preferential shopping access or, distribution networks are inefficient, social welfare cannot be optimal, even if the incomes shoppers earn precisely equals the values they add.

The Paretian standard is also helpful in evaluating the utility possibilities of economic systems. This is accomplished by mapping the Pareto ideal retail distribution point E in Figure 2.3 into utilities in the utility space shown in Figure 2.4. The coordinate axes array ordinal iso-utilities

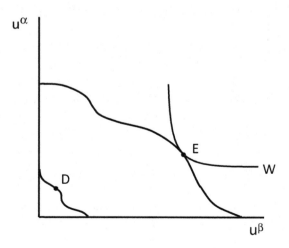

Figure 2.4   Pareto Utility Possibilities.

in increasing order from the origin, and points within the space identify the iso-utility level attained by each participant consuming his or her respective share of the retail distribution. The Pareto optimal utilities are those at point E, and can be complemented with a set of counterfactual utility optima derived variously by assuming different states of appreciation, or by redistributing equilibrium retail allotments. This set which takes account of compassionate welfare transfers is called the utility possibilities frontier (UPF) and can be compared with alternative utility feasibility frontiers (UFF) generated from points like E'' in Figure 2.2 and corresponding points like D' in Figure 2.3. A grand utility possibility frontier (GUPF) can also be computed that explores the impact of changes in the initial wealth distribution on factor allocation, production, distribution and redistribution.[5]

It should be obvious that ordinal utility states in inefficient systems are inferior to the Paretian ideal in every instance because they under-produce, manufacture dispreferred items with inferior characteristics, fail to optimally distribute supplies in the retail sector, and cannot efficiently redistribute given authoritarian priorities, and prevailing institutions. Instead of generating Pareto ideal utility at E, the non-Pareto systems only allow its citizens to achieve the iso-utilities shown at D.

Although point E is indisputably superior to D as both participants perceive their utility, there are other factors to be considered in appraising merit. Altruism or envy (inter-dependent utilities) which violates Pareto assumptions, if taken into account could modify utilitarian outcomes and welfare judgments about them. The complication can be expressed by redrawing the utility frontiers, or by constructing a separate welfare space where external observers evaluate the social merit of utilitarian outcomes given their own scale of values.[6] Alternatively, if analysts are solely interested

---

[5]The democratic competitive ideal can accommodate compassionate transfers of income and wealth through private charity or by empowering the government to serve as transfer agent. The Pareto equilibrium points in Figures 2.1–2.4 will vary with these income and wealth transfers. All will be achieved with the assistance of Walrasian and Marshallian automatic price and quantity adjustment mechanisms. Voluntary compassionate transfers, thus allow ideal democratic competitive systems to be as egalitarian or inegalitarian as citizens' desire.

[6]The value space can be a single vector, which assigns a scalar value to the Pareto optimal point E, and all counterfactual points along the utility possibilities frontier. The highest value of W will be best, even if it is associated with a utility score other than E.

in making judgments about the merit of inter-participant utility distributions, this can be illustrated with a nested set of Bergsonian social welfare contours shaped like community indifference curves, convex to the origin.[7] (See Appendix 1). If the judge prefers the competitive outcome, then the Bergsonian W will be tangent at point E.[8]

This conclusion also can be extended to the public sector. Elected government officials in principle can use markets where appropriate, and simulate ideal Paretian outcomes with optimal quantitative methods. Kenneth Arrow however has shown that democratic provision of public services is intrinsically inefficient because elected officials cannot completely ascertain individual desires through majority rule balloting;[9] a deficiency compounded whenever governments distribute services through administrative methods instead of through competitive markets.[10]

Ideal democratic competitive outcomes thus aren't necessarily superior. The Pareto standard is helpful, but seldom is the final word, even if competitive outcomes existed.[11]

---

[7] Abram Bergson (1938), "A Reformulation of Certain Aspects of Welfare Economics," *Quarterly Journal of Economics*, Vol. 52, No. 1, pp. 210–234.

[8] The Bergsonian welfare score at point E is indicated by the superscript value placed on the welfare curve tangent at E. If the judge, disprefers E, then there will be another Bergsonian welfare contour with a higher superscript value tangent at some point E' along the utility possibilities frontier. Although the example given stresses the utility distribution, Bergsonian welfare functions can include much finer judgments including the moral worth of every individual's consumption bundle, as well as welfare interdependencies. Judges also are free to consider other counterfactuals such as wealth reallocations, and the spiritual environment.

[9] This is called the "Arrow Paradox." Kenneth Arrow (1951). *Social Choice and Individual Values*, New York: Wiley; Abram Bergson (1938), "A Reformulation of Certain Aspects of Welfare Economics," *Quarterly Journal of Economics*, Vol. 52, No. 1, pp. 210–234.

[10] There are problems with Arrow's numerical demonstration. See Eric Maskin's introduction in Kenneth Arrow (2012). *Social Choice and Individual Values*, Princeton: Princeton University Press.

[11] There are a variety of practical indicators available for appraising systems merit, including Gini coefficients, the United Nation's Human Development Index, and Legatum index. See Corrado Gini (1921). "Measurement of the Inequality of Incomes," *The Economic Journal*, Vol. 31, pp. 124–126. Xu Kuan (2004). "How has the Literature on Gini's Index Evolved in the Past 80 Years?", *China Economic Quarterly*, Vol. 2, pp. 757–778; United Nations (2006). *The State of Human Development*, Available at http://hdr.undp.org; *The 2009 Legatum Prosperity Index: An Inquiry into Global Wealth and Wellbeing*, French president Nicolas Sarkozy created the Commission on the Measurement of Economic and Social

Disequilibrium Adjustment Mechanism

Figures 2.1–2.4 illustrate the characteristics of general equilibria where market participants exhaustively optimize their utility in work, production, distribution, transfers, and other pursuits. These results are attained through extensive, rational negotiations with other transactors influenced by prices (terms of exchange) and the requirements of profit maximization.

The search takes two basic forms depending on whether transactors negotiate the exchange of stocks (including inventories and labor), or the production of new manufactures. Both may involve profit seeking, but in the first case price adjustment is primary, and in the second output adjustment dominates.

The price negotiation processes is called the Walrasian excess demand, price adjustment mechanism in honor of Leon Walras (1834–1910), an eminent 19th century French general equilibrium theorist. It hypothesizes that if at any moment sellers perceive that their offer prices exceed buyers' willingness to pay (excess supply) leaving suppliers with excess inventories, they will respond by reducing their offer price. If the discount proves to be insufficient, they will continue cutting prices until their inventory holdings are optimal. Should they over-discount, they will swiftly discover that their inventories are too low. At this point, they will probe buyers' willingness to bid by raising prices, continuing to do so until supply and demand are equal.

The decision rules are simple. The market price (p) at any instant (t) is specified to be a function (F) of the difference between the quantity (q) demand (d) and the quantity supplied (s).

$$\mathrm{dp/dt} = F(q^d - q^s) \qquad (2.1)$$

If $q^d > q^s$, then

$\mathrm{dp/dt} > 0$; and prices will rise.

If $q^d < q^s$, then

$\mathrm{dp/dt} < 0$; and prices will fall.

Progress in 2008. The Commission issued an inaugural report 14 September, 2009, with some useful aspects, diminished by thinly veiled advocacy of Sarkozy's political agenda. See Robert Bate (2009), *What Is Prosperity and How Do We Measure It?* AEI online, Tuesday, 27 October.

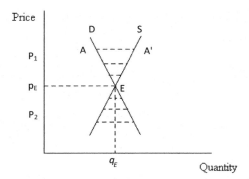

Figure 2.5   Walrasian Price Adjustment.

Both processes will continue until dp/dt = 0, which will be a stable equilibrium because the adjustment mechanism is symmetric. Both excess demand
and excess supply are automatically reduced to zero through a competitive
utility search.

Figure 2.5 provides a geometric version of the Walrasian process in the
retail market. Price is arrayed on the ordinate, quantity along the abscissa.
The demand curve is downward sloping in accordance with the principle of
diminishing marginal utility. The supply curve slopes upward because the
cost of stocking inventories increases with congestion. Consider the case
where the retailer is overstocked at point A'. The corresponding offer price
is p_1, which intersects the demand curve at A. Supply q^s exceeds demand,
q^d, which according to the Walrasian rule causes the retailer to discount
to p_2. Excess supply here diminishes, but the process isn't complete. Discounting continues to E, where demand and supply are equal. If the retailer
overshoots the mark, and over-discounts, the Walrasian process will work
in reverse, with prices rising until E is attained.

The Walrasian excess demand price adjustment mechanism causes capital and labor to be reallocated from R in Figure 2.1 to D. The wage rate at
R is too low compared with the rental rate on capital. This creates excess
demand for labor, which raises the wage, making it the same for both
employers. D is a counterfactual, not a true competitive equilibrium so the
process is incomplete, and will be modified further as profit seeking causes
the first output activity to contract, and the second to expand.

The Walrasian excess demand price adjustment mechanism also applies
in Figure 2.3. Here, bidding causes the price of good q_2 to rise, redistributing

the assortment of retail supplies from R to D, which again is a counterfactual equilibrium point. Then the ability of individuals A and B to pay, given their budget constraints derived from earned income in Figure 2.1, brings about the full equilibrium at *E*. There is no new production in the retail diagram. All goods sold were created at *E* in Figure 2.2.

Clearly, Walrasian price adjustment has broad scope, but it doesn't govern production. Prices also may vary in determining optimal supplies, but the driving force in the competitive model is profit maximization. As before, transactors are ultimately striving to augment their utility, but do so indirectly by increasing income (profit) and wealth. This process is called the Marshallian excess price, quantity adjustment mechanism after the British economist Alfred Marshall (1840–1924). In the most general case, manufacturers are assumed to know the buyers' demand curve. This allows them to compare the demand price they face for every level of production with the firm's corresponding unit cost. The difference is the excess price, that is, unit profit computed as the difference between unit revenue and cost.

The firm's decision rule is elementary. The quantity supplied (q) at any instant (t) is specified to be a function (G) of the difference between the demand price (p^d) and the unit production cost (p^s).

$$dq/dt = G(p^d - p^s) \qquad (2.2)$$

If $p^d > p^s$, then

$dq/dt > 0$, and firms will expand production.

If $p^d < p^s$, then

$dq/dt < 0$, and managers will curtail production.

Both process will continue until, $dq/dt = 0$, which will be a stable equilibrium because the adjustment mechanism is symmetric. Both excess quantities demanded, and excess quantities supplied are automatically reduced to zero through a competitive utility/profit maximization search.

Figure 2.6 provides a geometric version of the Marshallian process in manufacturing. Price is arrayed on the ordinate, quantity along the abscissa. The demand curve is downward sloping reflecting buyers' diminishing marginal utility. The supply curve slopes upward because the marginal physical productivity of inputs (valued at fixed prices) is a diminishing

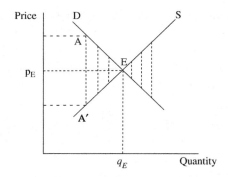

Figure 2.6   Marshallian Product Adjustment.

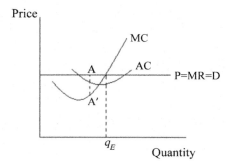

Figure 2.7   Profit Maximizing.

function of output. Consider the case where the firm discovers that for the achieved production level q_1, the demand price p_1 at A exceeds the supply price (marginal cost) p_2 at A'. The vertical difference means that the firm makes a unit profit, and according to the Marshallian rule expands production to q_2. A recalculation of the demand price and supply cost reveals that unit profit remains positive, and the search proceeds to q_E, where unit revenue (price) exactly equals unit supply cost. If the manager overshoots the mark, expanding production beyond E, the Marshallian process will work in reverse. The firm will discover that it is losing money on the production of each unit beyond q_E, and will return to E.

The soundness of the Marshallian principle can be confirmed with the conventional geometry of profit maximization illustrated in Figure 2.7. The variables on the ordinate and abscissa are the same, but the downward sloping demand curve has been replaced with an infinitely elastic marginal revenue curve in accordance with the perfectly competitive assumption that small firms cannot influence market prices. A marginal cost curve substitutes for the Marshallian supply curve, and an average variable cost curve is added for completeness. Suppose as before that at q_1, marginal revenue (A) exceeds marginal cost (A'). The difference between MR and MC is a unit profit that will encourage the firm to expand to q_2. Once again, unit profit is positive, and the manager will continue probing until equilibrium (profit maximization) is achieved at E. If there is a miscalculation, and the enterprise expands output to q_3, a loss will be incurred, prompting a return to E. The Marshallian principle and profit maximization thus come to the same thing, yielding the familiar conclusion that profit seeking governs managerial action in competitive economies.

Specifically, the Marshallian excess price, quantity adjustment mechanism causes both firms in Figure 2.1 to produce the optimal assortment and volumes of their respective goods. If, for example, the economy were operating at the counterfactual optimum D, profit seeking would cause firm 1 to expand, and firm 2 to contract production until the true equilibrium was achieved at E. Likewise, in Figure 2.2, firms operating on production feasibility frontiers will be driven to expand output along any vector until they reach the production possibility frontier, and then will be guided to E by a combination of Walrasian and Marshallian processes.

The invisible hand is the combination of both automatic adjustment mechanisms, or equilibration can be thought of as a two handed process, one Walrasian, the other Marshallian, often operating interactively.

The power of economic theory lies in its existence theorems which demonstrate the possibility of attaining E in all the figures under planned, competitive and mixed regimes, and further in the efficacy of the invisible hand. It is often claimed that planning and mixed methods are as good as, or even better than the invisible hand, but this is false. Planning and administrative methods are informationally and computationally inferior.

It should also be observed that the core competitive model not only is capable of achieving a global utility maximizing equilibrium at any instant, but can be extended to encompass the future. The same logic invoked to demonstrate the existence and competitive feasibility of static general equilibrium can be applied to investment, technology choice and hence, long term growth. The analysis reveals that the fastest growth rate isn't necessarily the best. As Irving Fisher (1867–1947) taught, investment is a device by which people can trade with the future. They don't simply invest. When people choose to save, they necessarily forego an equivalent amount of current consumption, in effect determining their preferred lifetime pattern of consumption. They can borrow to consume today, repaying out of future income, or can save to enjoy an augmented consumption stream. Either way, not only will a rational best economic outcome exist in the present, but in all futures too.

Chapter 3

Bounded Rationality

The Philosophes, forefathers of today's rational economic theorists, never claimed that human reason was divine or unbounded, contending only that normally distributed rational powers were sufficient to assure that every utility-seeker could realize his or her self-perceived potential.[1] This "warts and all" individualist standard is sensible and informs most modern discussions of complete optimization.

However, there have always been sound grounds for believing that the allowance Philosophes made for mundane human imperfections didn't adequately address their critics' objections; that they didn't sufficiently appreciate that human reason might be too feeble to justify Enlightenment claims. People sometimes are proverbially irrational. Many are "penny wise and pound foolish." Some are "spendthrifts" who think that it is thrifty to squander money. Others are "pinchpennies," "tightwads" and misers who hoard when they should be consuming. Likewise, people may be incapable of acting consistently (unable to construct consistent, comprehensive, monotonic, doubly differentiable utility preference functions), or their

---

[1]The leading thinkers of the Enlightenment in France were the Philosophes. These 18th-century literary men, scientists, and philosophers were sometimes far apart from one another in their personal views. However, they shared the belief that reason should be the ultimate authority in human affairs. This idea, called rationalism, was central to Enlightenment thought. The Philosophes expressed support for social, economic, and political reforms inspired by the philosophic thought of René Descartes, the skepticism of the libertarians, or freethinkers, and the popularization of science by Bernard de Fontenelle. In the early part of the 18th century, the movement was dominated by Voltaire and Montesquieu.

instincts, passions, intuitions and dementia may ride roughshod over their good judgment. Reason accordingly doesn't guarantee comprehensively ideal outcomes, an inference confirmed by psychoanalysis and psychiatry.

Contemporary realist neoclassical economists agree on comparatively narrow grounds, assigning pride of place for incomplete utility maximizing, profit maximizing and cost minimizing to informational and computational barriers.[2] It is sufficient from their perspective to suppose that while people are reasonable enough to solve a wide variety of complex problems, they cannot fully optimize because the task of constructing complete intertemporal utility hyper-surfaces for all conceivable choices is overwhelming. Moreover even if individuals succeed at any instant, their hyper-surfaces would become swiftly outdated, or the immense effort could prove superfluous when choosing whether to forego a scoop of vanilla ice cream for two scoops of chocolate at the margin. The bottom line here is that bounded rationality prevents consumers from completely utility optimizing, compelling them instead to sub-optimize where they can, employ heuristic (eclectic experience) methods where they can't in an effort to supplement utility, and satisfice in the sense of making do with the result.

The same principle holds if the definition of bounded rational is expanded beyond the neoclassical threshold to encompass causal and normative unknowability (paradox), deficient intellect, dis and misinformation, and psychological counterforces, while satisficing can be broadened to include cases where individuals refrain from completely utility-seeking because they are lazy or are willing to accommodate individuals or groups without thoroughly assessing costs and benefits.

The Philosophes' overestimation of reason's power is supported further by similar supply side difficulties that make satisficing versions of neoclassical theory more plausible than the optimizing norm. This entails some loss, but there is consolation. Bounded rationality narrowly construed strengthens neoclassical theory's realism without sacrificing the axiom of individual utility-seeking (as distinct from utility optimizing), and doesn't preclude sub-optimizing behavior.

---

[2]Herbert Simon (1957). "A Behavioral Model of Rational Choice," *Quarterly Journal of Economics*, 59, pp. 99–118. Simon (1957). *Models of Man*, New York. See this volume, Chapters 12–15.

Although imperfect, people in this softened neoclassical version of Enlightenment idealism are capable of learning and achieving superior results. Bounded rational and satisficing behavior aren't divine, nor do they constitute a full-fledged Kuhnian paradigm shift,[3] but they are widely considered pragmatic,[4] and provide the foundation for exploring many novel types of economic behavior excluded in the perfectly competitive framework.[5]

---

[3]Thomas Kuhn (1962). *The Structure of Scientific Revolutions*, Chicago: University of Chicago Press. A Kuhnian revolution requires both a new and a researchable paradigm. The concept of bounded rationality provides a new lens for rethinking economic organization and modern state governance.

[4]Pragmatism is a philosophically informed methodology for reconciling realism with unattainable idealist ends (including ideal paradox) to devise effective utility improving strategies. Charles Sanders Peirce, *Pragmatism as a Principle and Method of Right Thinking* (Lectures on Pragmatism 1903, edited by Patricia Turisi), Continuum International, 1997, Pierce, *Philosophy of Mathematics: Selected Writings*, Bloomington: Indiana University Press, 2010. Peirce (1985). *Historical Perspectives on Peirce's Logic of Science: A History of Science*, 2 Vols., Carolyn Eisele, ed., Mouton De Gruyter, Berlin, New York, Amsterdam. Edmund Arens and David Smith (1994). The Logic of Pragmatic Thinking: From Peirce to Habermas, Prometheus Books. Phyllis Chiasson (2001); *Peirce's Pragmatism: The Design for Thinking*, Amsterdam.

[5]The precise costs of satisficing can be clarified by combining Paul Samuelson's concept of "feasibility frontiers" with Herbert Simon's "bounded rationality" to appraise whether psychologically induced consumption and production inefficiencies and distortions are large or small? Samuelson assumes for didactic purposes that reason driven constrained optimization generates diversely constrained "second best" optimizing "feasibility frontiers" that are counterparts to ideal "possibility frontiers." Samuelson understands that these outcomes cannot be formally construed as equilibria (they are just observables) [see Paul Samuelson, "Optimal Compacts for Redistribution," in Samuelson, *Collected Scientific Papers*, Vol. 4, Chapter 257, MIT Press, Cambridge 1966], but argues nonetheless that the analogy helps visualize the essential characteristics of the second best. Constraints that affect productivity and/or the level of production are said to cause technical efficiency, measured by the distance of any observed point from its corresponding ideal on the possibility frontier. Those that affect input and product assortments and distributions are said to cause economic inefficiencies, meaning that forced substitution diminishes utility even if activities occur on possibility frontiers and more so when observables lie below possibilities.

Simon's psychological factors which are elements of Samuelson's larger constraint set have the same effects. However reflection shows that they are more damaging to the concept of optimizing than Samuelson acknowledges, implying that technical and economies inefficiencies are much more pronounced than Samuelson's narrative suggests.

These advances are welcome. Nonetheless, the realism of bounded rational neoclassical theory remains incomplete because it excludes sundry omitted psychological variables, satisficing and ideocratic behavior that cannot be accommodated within rational Enlightenment axioms.[6] Neoclassical theory no matter how it is re-conceptualized in Simon's terms can never be comprehensively realistic because it only addresses "rational selection" that ignores the construction of individual preferences. It disregards the full spectrum of satisficing behavior,[7] and excludes emotionally conflicted choice.

Simon's inefficiencies are intrinsic, not extrinsic. Utility-seeking isn't hampered by innocuous natural impediments. "Optimizing" is superseded by "satisficing." People cannot attain their ideal possibilities because their "rationality" is inadequate, and frequently subordinate to non-rational motivations. Where Samuelson's feasibility concept gives the impression that shortfalls from equilibrium in competitive market economies is apt to be consistent with the broad spirit of rational optimizing, Simon's feasibility by contrast challenges the logical foundations of positive and normative economic theory.

[6]Ideocratic is a term used by Martin Malia to describe ideologically guided government policy. It should not be confused with idiocratic, meaning idiotic governance as satirized in the 2006 cult film "Idiocracy." See Martin Malia (1994). *The Soviet Tragedy: A History of Socialism in Russia, 1917–1991*, The Free Press.

[7]If people are satisfied with bounded rational outcomes because they have thoroughly assessed the potential benefits of further utility searching, then this "satisficing" comes to the same thing as constrained optimization. People however, often satisfice without thoroughly investigating utility possibilities for diverse reasons. This behavior is never neoclassical and always realist or neo-realist.

Chapter 4

Core Consumer Behavior Theory: Ideal and Realist

Contemporary economic theory remains wedded to Enlightenment idealism, while gradually evolving in a realist direction that stops well short of an inclusive economic theory. The realist element relaxes presumptions about people's ability to optimally choose, and free enterprise's power to generate worthy outcomes, with or without state regulation. This has been accomplished by supplementing neoclassical Enlightenment idealist proofs with more realistic variants generating similar, but normatively ambiguous results across the spectrum of consumer, production, distribution, transfer, finance, and public service theory.

This chapter reviews core idealist neoclassical competitive consumption theory, identifies its vulnerable axioms, and provides realistic modifications, as a platform for later consideration of omitted psychological and ideocratic variables, as well as normative issues that need to be taken into account in inclusive economic theory.

Idealist Neoclassical Consumer Utility Theory

We begin with the ideal rationalist neoclassical concept of individual consumption in a competitive market economy. Everyone is postulated to be a consumer, and consumer spending drives the private sector. If a good or service is desirable, consumers will buy it at the right price. If either is unappealing, it will not be purchased, and production will cease. Consumers determine what will and will not be produced.

Economists recognizing these fundamentals pose two basic questions: Why do consumers desire goods and services? How do they decide what to buy?

Jeremy Bentham offered a well-argued hedonistic explanation in the late 18th century. He contended that consumption gives people "utility" (pleasure) and purchasing the right bundle of goods and services allows them to maximize utility (or net pleasure taking account of painful side effects), within their means.

Contemporary idealist neoclassical consumer theory embellishes this good start by relaxing Bentham's hedonism. It substitutes utility (usefulness) for the pleasure principle, and softens the self-centeredness of Bentham's individualism by acknowledging that consumer demand often is co-determined by various endogenous ethical and obligational factors including family duty.[1] Hedonism may be modified, or even subordinated to virtue ("virtue ethics")[2] and duty (deontology).[3] It also grapples with the troublesome problem of human imperfection by stressing the possibilities of learning.

Utility-seeking for modern idealist neoclassical consumer theorists consequently is elastic. It may mean complete hedonistic optimization in some cases and ethically constrained optimization in others. People are assumed to have the capacity and wit to fully determine their preferences, acquire the requisite information, and comprehensively rationally select. There is room for human error and learning, but otherwise, it is supposed

---

[1]Economists are aware of the issue, and it is implicitly encompassed by the relational variables in Bergson's concept of social welfare functions, but for the most part is treated as a special topic.

[2]Deidre McCloskey (2007). *The Bourgeois Virtues: Ethics for an Age of Commerce*, Chicago: University of Chicago Press. Kamm, F. M. (2007). *Intricate Ethics: Rights, Responsibilities, and Permissible Harm*. New York: Oxford University Press. Immanuel Kant (2005). *Groundwork of the Metaphysic of Morals*, New York: Harper and Row Publishers.

[3]Olson, Robert G. (1967) "Deontological Ethics", in Paul Edwards (ed.), *The Encyclopedia of Philosophy*, London: Collier Macmillan. Deontological ethics, or deontology (from Greek *deon*, "obligation, duty;" and logia) judges the morality of an action based on the action's adherence to a rule or rules. It is sometimes described as "duty" or "obligation" or "rule"-based ethics, because rules "bind you to your duty." Deontological ethics is commonly contrasted to consequentialism. Deontological ethics is also contrasted to pragmatic ethics. See Chapter 1.

that men and women comprehensively utility maximize generating optima that are Pareto, although not necessarily normatively best.

This sophisticated version of idealist neoclassical consumer utility theory has the virtue of generality, but is opaque in many important regards. Modeling cannot tell us whether consumers individually and collectively are really efficient, or make wise choices. The theory only stipulates that insofar as people are rational (an issue requiring verification), they will satisfy their desires as best as they can.

The formulation resonates because it accords with common sense and is flexible. Consumers find idealist neoclassical consumption theory plausible. They believe that they shop carefully and choose wisely, occasional errors notwithstanding. The contemporary concept of consumer utility appears sensibly nuanced, and economists seem content to leave the issue of externalities, psychological, ideocratic, and normative factors to others, but as will soon be demonstrated, this delegation comes at a steep price.[4]

Graphical Illustration

The fundamentals of ideal core consumer behavior theory, given these refinements, are easily elaborated. For simplicity, we begin with a diagrammatic approach that relies on a "utility surface" (see Figure 4.1) assuming that the consumer's preferences are well defined. The x_1 and x_2 axes show the quantities of two different goods. It does not matter what the goods are. One of them is measured along the x_1 axis and other along the x_2 axis. Suppose for narrative sake that x_1 is gasoline and x_2 is bread. Gallons of gasoline are measured on the x_1 axis and loaves of bread on the x_2 axis.

---

[4]Herbert Simon (1957). "A Behavioral Model of Rational Choice", in Simon (ed.), *Models of Man: Social and Rational-Mathematical Essays on Rational Human Behavior in a Social Setting*. New York: Wiley. Herbert Simon (1990). "A Mechanism for Social Selection and Successful Altruism," *Science*, Vol. 250, No. 4988, pp. 1665–1668. Herbert Simon (1991). "Bounded Rationality and Organizational Learning," *Organization Science*, Vol. 2, No. 1, pp. 125–134. Gerd Gigerenzer and Reinhard Selten (2002). *Bounded Rationality*. Cambridge: MIT Press. Ariel Rubinstein (1998). *Modeling Bounded Rationality*. MIT Press. Tisdell, Clem (1996). *Bounded Rationality and Economic Evolution: A Contribution to Decision Making, Economics, and Management*, Cheltenham, UK: Brookfield. Daniel Kahneman (2003). "Maps of Bounded Rationality: Psychology for Behavioral Economics," *The American Economic Review*, Vol. 93, No. 5, pp. 1449–1475.

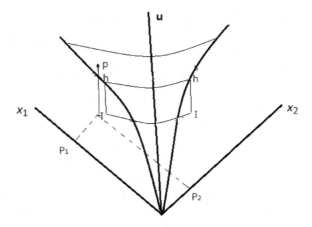

Figure 4.1   Utility Surface.

There is a third axis marked U. Utility is measured along this axis. A "utility surface" rises above the x_1x_2 plane. The height of the surface above x_1x_2 measures utility.

Look at the point marked p. It lies on the utility surface. Its height above the x_1x_2 plane measures the utility of p_1 gallons of gasoline and p_2 loaves of bread. Any point on the utility surface shows the utility of some combinations of gasoline and bread.

Now observe curve hh. It runs along the surface at a constant height above x_1x_2. It is an iso-utility surface tracing points with the same utility. If this curve is projected into the x_1x_2 plane, it still traces out the same combinations of x_1 and x_2 with the same utility. Curves like hh are called indifference curves. Each point on curve hh has the same utility.

Next consider Figure 4.2. There are three indifference curves in this diagram. There could be many more. Each height on the utility surface can produce an indifference curve. So theoretically, there is an infinity of indifference curves. They cover the x_1x_2 plane solidly.

Figure 4.3 displays some indifference curves and a straight line tangent to one of the indifference curves. The line shows the different combinations of x_1 and x_2 that the consumer can purchase. To locate the straight line, we divide the total amount of money that he can spend by the price of gasoline. This gives us the point at which the straight line intersects the x_1 axis, the gasoline axis. We also divide the amount of money by the price of a loaf

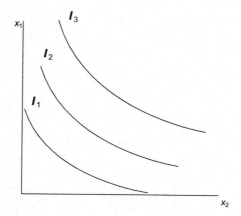

Figure 4.2   Indifference Curves.

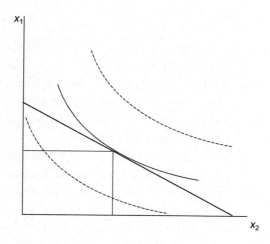

Figure 4.3   Budget Line.

of bread, giving us the point at which the line intersects the x_2 axis. If we connect the two points, we trace out all the combinations of gasoline and bread that the buyer can afford.

Which of these combinations of gasoline and bread will be chosen? The answer is the one that lies on the highest indifference curve and falls under or on his budget line. Why? Because it provides the highest level of

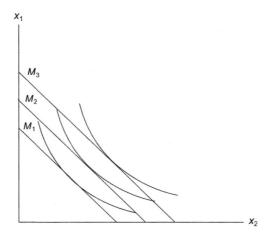

Figure 4.4   Money Budget Lines.

utility on the utility surface, that is, it maximizes consumer satisfaction and therefore is the buyer's "equilibrium point."

Inspect Figure 4.4. It shows three parallel "budget lines." These lines represent different amounts of money. M_2 shows more money than M_1, and M_3 shows more than either of the two. The budget lines are parallel because the prices of gasoline and bread have not changed.

What happens if the price of one of the goods changes? Figure 4.5 provides the answer. It shows that the price of bread declined moving the budget line from the B_1 position to the B_2 position. The consumer can buy more bread at the lower price.

We could trace out an "individual demand schedule" by considering a sequence of prices for bread or gasoline, or if we replaced it with an "individual demand curve," a graph showing the amount of bread that the individual would buy at different prices. By doing this for all the individuals in a market and adding the amounts at each price, we obtain a "market" demand schedule, and market demand curve.

Market demand is particularly interesting because it is used in policy questions, business problems, and other types of applications, but cannot be separated from individual demand. Understanding individual demand consequently is essential for correctly interpreting applied economic issues.

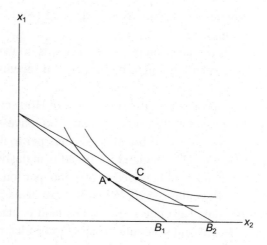

Figure 4.5   Relative Price Change.

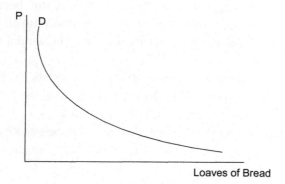

Loaves of Bread

Figure 4.6   Market Demand Curve.

Figure 4.6 illustrates a market demand curve. It is negatively sloped because as shown in Figure 4.5, individuals will buy more of a good as the price declines. The shape of the market demand curve mimics the responses of individuals to price change.

Money

If the price of a good falls, the quantity sold increases. Does the total revenue from the sale of the good increase or decrease? The lower price would reduce the revenue but the larger quantity sold would increase the revenue. Which will dominate?

The answer depends on the circumstances. There is no general rule. If the revenue increases, demand is said to be "elastic." If revenue decreases, demand is "inelastic."

To illustrate this, suppose that in the small town of Horsechester, North Dakota, when bread is priced at 80 cents per loaf, 100 loaves will be sold each day. The revenue is $80. But if bread is 70 cents per loaf, 110 loaves will be sold. The revenue is $77. Demand for bread is inelastic.

But suppose that when bread is priced at 60 cents per loaf, 150 loaves will be sold every day. Revenue is $90. When it is 50 cents per loaf, 270 loaves will be sold per day. Revenue is $135. Demand is elastic. Thus, it is possible for the same demand schedule or curve to be elastic in one part and inelastic in another.

The demand curve in Figure 4.6 illustrates this. It is inelastic in the left part of the curve and elastic in the right part. This is true because in the left part, it is steep. As price declines, it does not induce much increase in quantity sold. The right part is flatter indicating a substantial increase in sales when price falls.

There is another way of looking at demand and elasticity. Elasticity is a comparison of the proportionate change in price with the proportionate change in quantity sold. We are comparing $\frac{\delta p}{p_1}$ with $\frac{\delta x}{x_1}$.

Assuming that the good is normal, one term will be negative. They are compared by using:

$$\frac{\frac{\delta x}{x_{j1}}}{\frac{\delta p_j}{p_{j1}}} = \frac{\delta x_j p_{j1}}{x_{j1}\delta p_j} = \eta_{jj}.$$

This is called the elasticity coefficient and it is negative. It shows the relative sizes of the proportionate quantity change and the proportionate price change. If

$$-1 < \eta_{jj} < 0,$$

then demand is inelastic. The proportionate price change is large compared to proportionate quantity change. If

$$\eta_{jj} < -1,$$

then demand is elastic. If

$$\eta_{jj} = -1,$$

then elasticity is unitary.

Recall that

$$-2 < -1.$$

The Horsechester data has two intervals:

x	p	and	p	x
0.8	100		0.6	150
0.7	110		0.5	270

For the first interval

$$\frac{\delta x}{x_1} \frac{p_1}{\delta p} = \frac{10}{100} \frac{0.8}{-0.1} = \frac{8}{-10} = -0.8$$

For the second interval

$$\frac{\delta x}{x_1} \frac{p_1}{\delta p} = \frac{120}{150} \frac{0.6}{-0.1} = \frac{72}{-15} = -4.8$$

The first interval is inelastic and the second is very elastic.

Vulnerable Assumptions

The theory of ideal utility maximization in the two commodity case beneficial to individuals and the community (Pareto optimality) elaborated above
seems compelling, but depends on the validity of seven vulnerable behavioral assumptions. Consumers are postulated: (1) to possess **well-defined
continuous preferences**, (2) that are **interpersonally independent**,[5] (3) to
rationally select, (4) to **exhaustively utility search** (optimizing rather than
satisficing), (5) to **autonomously choose** (individuals and households),

---

[5]The independence of interpersonal utilities is essential to assure that preferences are
judiciously formed for each individual, and that preferences are stable enough to allow
optimization processes to reach completion. These issues are sometimes addressed in
"adaptive" economic theory. John Gross (2008). *The Theory of Adaptive Economic Behavior*,
Cambridge: Cambridge University Press.

(6) to act **ethically (competitively)** within the framework of a Lockean social contract, and (7) **well-being is solely determined by successive rational marginal choices**.[6] Another vulnerable assumption: (8) **rational preference formation** (including interpersonal utilitarian accommodation) requires attention, but consideration is deferred to Part II.

The critical assumptions of independent well-defined continuous preferences, rational selection, exhaustive utility searching, autonomous choice, and ethical conduct do not seem too stringent at first glance subject to the usual caveats about imperfect judgment, suggesting that the sum of all individual consumer utilities is more or less easily achieved. However, close inspection reveals that the task is so daunting that few if any individuals are capable of utility maximizing in the idealist sense, a point easily confirmed by pondering the mathematical complexities (see Appendix 2).

The softness of the ideal inference moreover is vivified further as soon as we take a modest step toward realism acknowledging that a large share of purchases is made collectively by households with conflicting preferences. The central problem is that while it is easy to visualize an ideal utility surface for an individual,[7] it is difficult to imagine how the similarly ideal utilities of family members should be combined into a single utility surface.[8]

---

[6]This is a weak definition of ethics that leaves ample room for normative debate.

[7]Visualization is easy, but practical estimation is elusive.

[8]The absence of a theory of family demand has frequently been noted in passing in economic literature, but there seems to be no development or extensive discussion of this subject, because as previously noted, interpersonal utility is incommensurable. For example, Samuelson once wrote:

> ... what is a man? Or a consumer? I am not so much concerned with the problem of Dr. Jekyll and Mr. Hyde but with the problem of Dr. Jekyll and Mrs. Jekyll. Much consumption behavior is family rather than individual behavior. Now a family must be quite sophisticated indeed to end up with a consistent set of collective preferences: e.g. if they set up the rule that the wife will always spend 99 percent (or 50 percent) of the income on her needs and the husband 1 percent (or 50 percent) on his quite different needs, this will not be consistent with an integrable set of price ratio elements. Only if the family acts in terms of a Bergson Social Welfare Function will this condition result. But to explain this further would take me into the frontier of research in welfare economics. (Samuelson's emphasis) Paul Samuelson (1950). "The Problem of Integrability in Utility Theory," *Economica*, Vol. 17, pp. 255–285.

This difficulty is compounded if we drop the idealist assumptions that consumer demand functions are transitive (consistent) and collectively additive; that is, if there are three sets of goods: A, B, and C, and if B is preferred to A, and C is preferred to B, then C must be preferred to A both for individuals and families.

Superficially, given the fundamental Enlightenment premise that consumers are rational (act coherently in their own interest), transitivity appears to be a completely acceptable foundation stone for the theory of individual demand, and collective demand that assumes additivity. However, it has not stood up well in experimental tests,[9] because individual consumers sometimes miscalculate, their preferences are incomplete and unstable, and collectives cannot agree on what should be their ideal composite set of continuously transitive preferences. Tests involving multidimensional choices such as vectors or set of goods sometimes yield intransitive results.[10]

Realist Reformulation of Consumer Utilitarian Choice

Both the individual and collective transitivity problems can be satisfactorily resolved, but only by dropping the idealist requirement that individuals and collectives completely and independently maximize their utility. This concession is unavoidable from a realistic standpoint, but nonetheless is

---

[9]K.O. May (1954). "Intransitivity, Utility and the Aggregation of Preference Patterns," *Econometrica*, Vol. 22, pp. 1–13. A. Tversky (1969). "Intransitivity of Preferences," *Psychological Review*, Vol. 26, pp. 31–48.

[10]For a further discussion of this, as well as other difficulties in applying optimization theory to economics, see F. Laville (2000). "Should We Abandon Optimization theory? The Need for Bounded Rationality," *The Journal of Economic Methodology*, Vol. 7, pp. 395–426.

Transitivity is a property or a characteristic that is possessed by any collection of objections or concepts that possess numbers. That is, objects or concepts that can be numbered or, it might be said, can be counted or measured. Confusion about transitivity arises when it is applied to a collection that is not countable or measurable and does not present a meaningful measurability.

To illustrate transitivity, let us first consider odd integers. We will consider small positive odd integer. For example, this sequence 1, 3, 5, 7, 9 . . . , 27. We now say in this set of numbers, we note that $17 > 15$ and; then $19 > 17$ and we know that, because of transitivity that, every positive odd number guarantees 19 is also greater than 17, or with reference to the specific set of any numbers.

Kenneth Arrow points out that social states need not be transitive.

unfortunate because it means that consumer efficiency cannot be reliably deduced solely on the presumption of unbounded human intellect.

Local Nonsatiation

The cloud over individual consumer transitivity can be lifted by dropping the assumption of continuously and consistently ordered preference functions in favor of a more realistic assumption sometimes called "local nonsatiation." This axiom says that for any chosen vector of goods, there always exists a more desired vector that can be reached by an increase of income or the fall of a price or prices. The principle was first used to sidestep transitivity by Sonnenschein in a more abstract and sophisticated mathematical setting than is used here.[11]

Local nonsatiation, which is a more flexible requirement than monotonicity,[12] permits utility seekers to terminate their searches without optimizing, maximizing, or achieving global satiation when human limitations prevent them from achieving their utilitarian potential. The local aspect illuminates how it is possible for rational individuals to make intransitive choices when they are prevented from searching the entire opportunity set. The seemingly irrational choice of A may not be unreasonable if local constraints make C seem inferior. Rational consumers always will choose C when nonsatiation is global, but in some local environments, they will not. Selecting A may merely reflect a local constraint (physical or temporary), not inconsistency.

Herbert Simon includes this type of constraint in a broader class called bounded rationality,[13] which he characterized 20 years ago as:

> The term (bounded rationality) was introduced about thirty years ago to focus attention upon the discrepancy between the perfect rationality that is assumed in

---

[11]H. Sonnenschein (1971). "Demand Theory without Transitive Preferences," in J.S. Chipman *et al.* (eds.), *Utility, Preference and Demand: A Minnesota Symposium*, New York: Harcourt Brace Jovanovich, pp. 215–223.

[12]It places no restrictions on the quantities of the goods in the two vectors or on the goods included. Goods not present in one vector may be present in another. For a discussion of this axiom, see Geoffrey Jehle, G.A. and Philip Reny (1998). *Advanced Microeconomic Theory*, Boston: Addison Wesley.

[13]Core consumer theory seldom if ever discusses mentally and spiritually transformative aspects of rational choice. This lacunae will be addressed in Chapter 13.

classical and neoclassical economic theory and the reality of human behavior as it is observed in economic life. The point was not that people are consciously and deliberately irrational, although they sometimes are, but that neither their knowledge nor their powers of calculation allow them to achieve the high level of optimal adaptation of means to ends that is posited in economics.

It is not enough to point out that some empirically erroneous assumptions underlie economic theory. In addition (a point for which Milton Friedman has argued), it is also necessary to show that it makes a difference — that we would reach different conclusions in our economic analyses if we substituted the concept of bounded rationality for the concept of global optimization. It is also necessary to show how assumptions of bounded rationality could replace assumptions of optimization in actual economic reasoning. (Simon's emphasis.)[14]

Simon observed further that substantial progress toward a positive theory of bounded rationality has been made in the field of artificial intelligence by using knowledge developed in the field of cognitive psychology.

We know today that human reasoning, the product of bounded rationality, can be characterized as selective search through large spaces of possibilities. The selectivity of the search, hence its feasibility, is obtained by applying rules of thumb, or heuristics, to determine which paths should be traced and which ones can be ignored. The search halts when a satisfactory solution has been found, almost always long before all alternatives have been examined.

These basic points about bounded rationality, which do not cover all cases of ostensible intransitivity,[15] can be employed to show how family demand (the collective transitivity problem) can be realistically determined for practical purposes even though the solutions are incomplete from an ideal theoretical perspective.

The word, family, is used in its usual meaning except that for the sake of generality individuals who live alone and have an income, earned or otherwise, that they may allocate as they wish are also considered to be families. Thus, when the word family is used, it includes one-person families unless they are specifically excluded.

---

[14]Herbert Simon (1992). "Introductory Comment" in M. Egidi and R. Marris (eds.), *Economics, Bounded Rationality and the Cognitive Revolution*, New York: Edward Elgar, pp. 3–7.
[15]We will see that in some cultures like Japan, people do not have fixed preferences. They substitute group preferences for their own when context makes this obligatory.

How does a family dispose of its income? We should note first that many decisions about spending in any pay period were made in the past. The rent or mortgage payment must be met. The payments into the tax-sheltered saving plan and insurance premiums must be made. Credit card bills and so on have to be paid. But the entire income is not usually used for these recurring charges.

How is the remaining income allocated? The families consider various possibilities that would yield vectors or sets of goods that, including recurring charges, fall within the family income, and choose the vector of goods that is considered most desirable. Since the family is already committed to recurring charges, it is really considering only the part of the goods vectors (bundles) that can be altered or eliminated.

How will they compare the vectors? They will not bring forward a utility measurement for each vector, nor will they rank all of them. They will choose the one that seems best by comparing it with each of a small number of other vectors. Once a vector is found to be inferior in a comparison, it is not compared to the others to obtain a ranking of all vectors; it is simply abandoned. In other words, they will choose the winner but they will not award a second place, a third place, and so on. Since they are not compiling an ordering or ranking of all vectors, transitivity is automatically excluded.

This description shows the essential process of choice, but does not place it in context. To do so, consider a family that has recently been formed, a newly married couple. Their first efforts at forming a budget will surely be tentative. But a little experience will allow them to discover more satisfactory ways of spending their money. They will find the affordable purchases that they like, including expenditures over and above recurring expenditures. Once they are satisfied with a budget, they will probably stay with it, thus establishing a habitual pattern of expenditures.

Nonetheless, it is a habitual pattern that is subject to change. Marginal changes may be made. A preferred substitute for a good may be found, or a new product may be purchased. Tastes change over time.

Of course, not all assortment changes are small. Shifts in income and wealth may have major impacts, including those associated with life's milestones. Aging alters needs and resources. The birth of a child or the deterioration of the health likewise strongly effect people's choices.

Families might respond by comprehensively reexamining their possibilities, but more realistically they evaluate how changes in purchasing power affect the desirability of purchasing a few strategic goods.

How do families determine that the purchase of one new goods vector is better than another. For a one-person family, there is presumably no problem. An individual can choose the vector that pleases her more than the others that she considers (given bounded rationality).

For a family consisting of more than one person, some decision protocol is needed.[16] Perhaps, a family has a consumption dictator, one person who decides what will be bought for each family member. More likely, the choice is the result of discussion and compromise among members of the family. In a family with small children, the parents will usually decide what should be bought for the children, taking into account the children's wishes. The process used by the family is not of central importance for the purposes at hand.[17] What is important is that the family, by whatever process, makes a decision and acts on it.

There are subtleties that should be noted. First, savings are treated as a good. From the standpoint of the economy as a whole, savings are, and should be, viewed as abstention from consuming, but from the viewpoint of the family, they are a disposition of income and thus similar to other disposition of income; the money has been spent to purchase savings and is no longer available. Thus, savings may be viewed as a good that the family may buy.[18]

Second, rules of thumb are routinely employed as acceptable surrogate decision criteria for "selective search through large spaces of possibilities.[19] Heuristics (experience-based techniques) permit the exclusion of many possibilities and the discovery of various satisfactory, but seldom

[16]Gary Becker (1993). *A Treatise on the Family*, Cambridge MA: Harvard University Press. Gary Becker (1962). "Irrational Behavior and Economic Theory," *Journal of Political Economy*, Vol. 70, No. 1, pp. 1–13.

[17]Theodore Bergstrom (2008). "The Rotten Kid Theorem," *The New Palgrave Dictionary of Economics*, London: Macmillan. http://www.dictionaryofeconomics.com/dictionary.

[18]Cf. Irving Fisher (1974). *The Theory of Interest*, Clifton, New Jersey: Augustus M. Kelley (originally published in 1930).

[19]Herbert Simon (1992). "Introductory Comment" in M. Egidi and R. Marris (eds.), *Economics, Bounded Rationality and the Cognitive Revolution*, New York: Edward Elgar, pp. 3–7.

optimal solutions. The family's decision process confronts member with millions of possible vectors of goods. The great majority however can be eliminated immediately by two simple heuristics. Goods vectors that cost more than the family income can afford (including credit) are excluded and those entailing a lower standard of living are disregarded.

Other possibilities are rejected *ad hoc*. Brother cannot have the rifle he wants because his parents believe that guns are dangerous and do not want one in the house. Sister cannot have the gold chain and gold bracelet she wants because it is bad taste for a girl of her age to wear expensive jewelry. The family will eat very little "red meat" because Mother considers it unhealthful. There are innumerable *ad hoc* heuristics; however, in practice, a few key rules seem to prevail. Dangerous goods, goods in bad taste, and unhealthful goods are disregarded, and many goods are purchased because other people expect us to have them.

The realist solution to family demand can be illustrated more formally as follows.

Assume that selection involves three goods. x_i is the quantity of the ith good purchased. δx_i is the amount of a change in ith good. Its price is denoted by p_i and a change in the price by δp_i.

We say that $\delta p_i \delta x_i < 0$ shows that the ith good is normal. If the price of i increases, the amount bought falls $\delta p_i > 0$ and $\delta x_i < 0$, hence $\delta p_i \delta x_i < 0$. Or if $\delta p_i < 0$, then $\delta x_i > 0$. This is what one expects for many goods.

If $\delta p_i \delta x_i > 0$ we have an inferior good. If the price decreases, less will be bought because some other good or goods are preferred. If the price increases, more will be bought of the good because other goods are now not available since more must be spent on good i. Therefore: $\delta p_i \delta x_i > 0$.

If $\delta p_i \delta x_i = 0$, the same quantity of the goods will be purchased regardless of price change. This is a satiety good. There are goods that will be purchased in whatever amount is needed regardless of price change. In prosperous households, the housewife will not change the quantity of salt used because the price goes up a little.

To what extent does the realist utility search replicate the ideal one?

Considering ideal core theory (complete consumer utility seeking assuming the continuity and transitivity of consumer preferences), it may be observed that it allows theorists to explain how income changes affect consumer purchases. Is the realist alternative equally powerful?

To assess this question, we make use of the family's budget equation in two consecutive time periods. The budget equation for the first time period is shown as

$$\sum_{i=1}^{n} p_{i1}x_{i1} = m_1. \tag{4.1}$$

Here, p_{i1} is the price of good i in period 1 and x_{i1} is its quantity, while m_1 is the amount of money the family has to spend in the first time period.

If the family experiences a change of income in period 2, we may write

$$m_2 = m_1 + \delta m. \tag{4.2}$$

We consider the case where $\delta m > 0$. Now local nonsatiation requires that a vector of goods preferred to that of period 1 be available. Hence, we say

$$x_{i1} + \delta x_{i1} = x_{i2}, \quad \forall i, \tag{4.3}$$

where δx_i represents the change in quantity of good i as the family adjusts to the new more preferred goods vector, and may be zero, but not all δx_i can be zero. Making use of (4.1)–(4.3) and noting that prices are unchanged we have

$$\sum_{i=1}^{n} p_{i1}x_{i1} + \sum_{i=1}^{n} p_1 \delta x_i = m_2 = m_1 + \delta m.$$

Ignoring the left-side equation and using (1) we have, after obvious manipulations,

$$\delta m = \sum_{i=1}^{n} p_{i1} \delta x_i. \tag{4.4}$$

Because $\delta m > 0$, (4) shows that positive quantity changes must dominate the summation. But some quantity changes may be zero. For example, an income increase for families above the subsistence level would not induce them to buy more table salt and other similar "satiety goods."

Some quantity changes could also be negative, i.e., inferior goods may be present. But these cannot be as large in their effects as those of the non-inferior goods.

A basic demand relation, that income changes and consumption changes are associated positively in the case of normal goods, which are neither inferior nor satiety goods, appears in (4.4). The budget constraint shows this without the presence of a utility function.

If, on the other hand, the income change is negative, then quantity decreases must dominate. The left side of (4.4) shows the amount of money that must be foregone while the right side shows the value of the goods that must be given up. Satiety goods and inferior goods may appear.

It may also be noticed that new goods can be introduced and old goods can be excluded very easily in (4.4). If good j, not purchased in period 1, is bought in 2, $x_{j1} = 0$ then $\delta x_j = x_{j2}$ and $\delta x_{j2} > 0$. If a good bought in 1 is not bought in 2, then $x_{k1} > 0$ and $\delta x_k = -x_{k1}$ and, of course, $x_{k2} = 0$.

Another advantage of the ideal core approach is that it shows the effects of a change of the price of one good on all goods. This can also be done in the present framework.

When the price of one good changes, the quantities of other goods may also change. Consequently, the family budget equation in period 2 may be shown as

$$\sum_{i=1}^{n} p_{i1}(x_{i1} + \delta x_i) + x_{j2}\delta p_j = m_2. \tag{4.5}$$

Here, the price of j changes. Noting that $\delta m = 0$ and using (1) and (2), we may write

$$x_{j2}\delta p_j = -\sum_i p_{i1}\delta x_i, \tag{4.6}$$

Or

$$(x_{j1} + \delta x_j)\delta p_j + p_{j1}\delta x_j = -\sum_{k \neq j} p_{k1}\delta x_k. \tag{4.7}$$

This shows the changes of the purchase of good j on the left and the changes in other goods on the right. Before analyzing (4.7) directly, we establish a background for the analysis.

The three kinds of goods mentioned earlier can be classified according to the family's response to changes in the price of the good. If $\delta p_j \delta x_j < 0$, we say that j is a normal good. If $\delta p_j \delta x_j > 0$, we say that j is an inferior good. If $\delta p_j \delta x_j = 0$, we say j is a satiety good, where $\delta p_j \neq 0$ in all three cases.

To illustrate this, we consider a decline in the price of j. Clearly, it is true that

$$(x_{j1} + \delta x_j)\delta p_j < 0.$$

Therefore, we can write

$$\delta x_j \delta p_j < -x_{j1}\delta p_j.$$

The right side must be positive. Consequently, $\delta x_j \delta p_j$ may be negative, positive, or zero. Thus, j can be a normal, inferior, or satiety good. A comparable demonstration can be made for a price increase.

We now turn to a closer examination of (4.7). Assume, for specificity, a price decrease. Consider the case of a satiety good; $\delta p_j < 0$ and $\delta x_j = 0$. The left side of (4.7) reduces to $x_{j1}\delta p_j$ which shows the reduction of spending on j and which, of course, is negative. The right side also must be negative to maintain the equality and this requires that the δx_k values must be predominantly positive, i.e., they must be positive in sufficient number and amounts to make the summation negative. Thus, the effect of a satiety good price decrease is to increase the use of other goods.

Next consider the case of an inferior good in which $\delta p_j < 0$ and $\delta x_j < 0$. Looking at the left side of (4.7), we note that the quantity in parentheses cannot be negative because negative consumption is not defined and would usually be positive, but could be zero. Thus, the first term in (4.7) is negative or zero and the second term is negative. Hence, the left side must be negative. Consequently, the $\delta x_k s$ in the summation on the right must be predominantly positive. Hence, lowering the price of an inferior good, increases the purchases of other goods.

The normal good case, where $\delta p_j < 0$, $\delta x_j > 0$, presents more complications than either the satiety or inferior cases. Looking at the left side of (4.7), it is clear that one term, the first one, is negative while the second is positive and consequently, we cannot give a sign to the left side. This ambiguity arises because the price has decreased and the quantity has, at the same time, increased. The question therefore arises regarding which term has the larger effect on the amount spent on good j. This same issue is posed in the idealist framework and is solved by invoking the concept of elasticity of demand with respect to the goods' own price.

We can adopt the same approach. Looking at (4.7), we can see that by multiplying δp_j through and then dividing the entire equation by $\delta p_j x_{j1}$, we get

$$1 + \frac{\delta x_j - \delta p_j}{\delta p_j x_{j1}} + \frac{p_j \delta x_j}{\delta p_j x_{j1}} = -\sum_{k \neq j} \frac{p_{k1} \delta x_p}{\delta p_j x_{j1}},$$

or

$$1 + \frac{\delta x_j}{x_{ji}} + \eta_{jj} = -\sum_{k \neq j} \frac{p_{k1} \delta x_p}{\delta p_j x_{j1}}. \qquad (4.8)$$

Looking at the right side of (4.8), we see that $\delta p_j < 0$, since we considered a price decline. We also note that the minus sign precedes the entire right side and we also know that the δx_k values are negative. How do we know this?

We know that when the price of good j fell, more of good j was purchased. The money to make this additional purchase came from buying less of some other goods, and the goods indexed by k represent the other goods of which less was bought. Thus, $\delta x_k < 0$.

There are three negatives multiplied into each term in the summation of the right side. Therefore, the right side is negative.

If the right side is negative, the left side must be negative to maintain the equality. We know that $1 + \frac{\delta x_j}{x_{j1}}$ is positive, because everything in it is positive, therefore $\eta_{jj} < 0$, which we could also tell by looking at its definition.

We know more than that; we know that $1 + \frac{\delta x_j}{x_{j1}}$ would often be only a little bit more than 1. In other words, $\frac{\delta x_j}{x_{j1}}$ would often be a small fraction, say 1/10 or less. Thus, for the left side of (4.8) to be negative, we must have $\eta_{jj} < -1$, but perhaps not much less. In other words, demand must be elastic but often not very elastic if the left side of (4.8) is to be negative.

The foregoing discussion of price change effects is phrased in terms of a price decline but a price increase could have been employed and analyzed in the same way with corresponding results obtained. The only difference involves a satiety good. Goods such as table salt, catsup, laundry detergent, and many others are not likely to have their family rate of consumption altered by a price increase. But there are some goods that might be satiety goods in the presence of a price fall that would be normal goods in the face of a price increase. These are expensive goods like steak, lobster, or salmon. The family might believe that it was getting enough protein so a fall in the price of steak would not induce it to purchase more steak. But they might feel that a rise of the price of steak made it so expensive that they should reduce its consumption for economic rather than dietary reasons.

This possibility does not present any problems in the present analysis. If the price of steak falls and the rate of consumption remains unchanged, it is a satiety good; if it rises and consumption declines, it is a normal good. Each is accommodated by the theory being advanced and thus presents no problems. That is, the fact that a good is a satiety good in one circumstance and a normal good under different conditions poses no difficulties.

It follows directly that relaxing key assumptions of ideal core theory,[20] particularly (1) the continuity and transitivity (utility numbers assigned to the various vectors must be transitive) of consumer preferences (utility functions are continuous, twice differentiable, and monotonic), (2) the independence of interpersonal utilities (a corollary of incompletely defined preference functions), (3) the completeness of utility search and even (4) the completeness of rational choosing fundamentally alters behavioral expectations in only two ways. First, it drops the presumption that reason, consistency, and self-discipline assure that individual utility outcomes (whatever utility may actually mean) are idealistically best (reason makes humans gods).[21] This implication extends to government entitlements and

---

[20]Ideal theory rests on either a utility function or an ordering of the vectors. If a utility function is used, it must be continuous, twice differentiable, and monotonic. It must be transitive in the sense that the utility numbers assigned to the various vectors must be transitive. If an ordering is used, it must also display transitivity. In either case, logical or mathematical conditions are imposed on the consumers without being justified as empirically appropriate restrictions.

[21]The realistic bounded rationality approach is based on the process of searching of possibilities spaces as expounded by Simon. This describes a psychological process and method of choice but it does not choose a certain alternative from a specified set of alternatives. Rather, it leaves to the family the decision as to what choices should be made. Thus, while it describes the process by which the choices are to be made, it does not impose logical or mathematical restrictions on the decision. And it proceeds from cognitive psychology

other transfers. Second, it leaves unsettled just how far real behavior and outcomes including competitiveness in the private and public consumption sectors depart from ideal potential.[22] Attempts have been made to gloss this ambiguity by assuming that consumption behavior is mostly rational, that people are not occasionally obliged to substitute group preferences for their own (forced preference substitution), that the interdependence of utilities is a minor matter, and that the "boundedness" of "bounded rationality" is not too restrictive. Real outcomes accordingly are often characterized as "second best," implying that even though they are imperfect, "workably competitive" markets still generate very good results. This may be so, and by extension, it also may be true that workably competitive markets are superior to alternative economic mechanisms, and consequently that small government is best, but these surmises do not follow rigorously from realist consumption theory. Poorer anticompetitive results are possible, even before considering omitted variables including serendipitous and extra-market experiences, illusions, delusions, fuzzy identities, culturally

---

which has an empirical basis. In addition, the bounded rationality approach uses local non-satiation, which says that a superior vector always exists that will be chosen if income and price changes permit. This would seem to have an obvious empirical basis.

Further, the realistic bounded rationality approach does not use the concept of exhaustive, comprehensive utility. Of course, it assumes that individuals and families have preferences but it does not extend the notion of preferences or utility beyond an immediate comparison; it does not make use of an overall rationality. In other words, it makes use of local nonsatiation, a weak assumption compared to those underlying the mainstream approach. It does not require the ideal, strictly consistent choice behavior of the mainstream, but it is compatible with such behavior if and when it does occur. It does not require the presence of a utility scale.

[22]Comparing results of the two approaches also shows important differences. Ideal consumer theory, as was noted above, shows the results of a price or an income change on the purchase made by an individual. So also does realistic bounded rationality. Ideal core theory produces individual demand equations. Realistic bounded rationality shows the amount of a good purchased by an individual or a family at any price and at any income level, thus also providing a theoretical basis for market demand equations. It accommodates the introduction of new goods more easily than does the mainstream. It also handles saving and debt in a simple, straightforward way, and does something that the conventional theory cannot do: It offers a theory of family demand. Moreover, and most importantly, it dispels the unwarranted inference that consumer behavior is normatively ideal from every individual's perspective, and by extension that social welfare is maximal in this same sense because the realistic approach makes no implicit judgment about the efficiency of individual's utility searches, or whether the searches of some are superior to those of others.

imposed obligations in an imperfectly competitive and collectively governed environment. Realist consumer theory, which relies on heuristics in other words, provides guidance on larger issues, but like any rule of thumb should be applied cautiously for inclusively assessing how best to foster human well-being, fulfillment, and contentment.

Summary

Idealist neoclassical consumer utility theory is vulnerable on six fundamental grounds: the assumptions of (1) **well-defined continuous preferences**, (2) **interpersonally independent preferences**, (3) **exhaustive utility searching**, (4) **rational selection**, (5) **autonomous choice**, (6) **virtuous pro-competitive ethical conduct**, and (7) **well-being's sole determination by successive rational marginal choices**. The analysis of autonomous choice exposes the implausibility of the existence of independent well-defined continuous preferences and exhaustive utility searching in household settings. The realist solution to these flaws is the concept of local nonsatiation. The concept enables theorists to reformulate core idealist neoclassical principles of rational, workably competitive, beneficial consumer utility-seeking in terms of heuristic satisficing protocols. This salvages the principle of rational utility searching in a soft form, but does not provide any guidance about the wisdom of each and every heuristic protocol. There is another fundamental assumption that is also vulnerable and warrants serious attention: (8) **rational preference formation** that is the foundation stone of neo-realist economic theory. Its significance will be explored in Part III.

Chapter 5

Production and Costs

Contemporary production and cost theory mimics the logic of consumption theory, which should hardly be surprising because production is a derived aspect of utility seeking. The ideal version assumes that producers without external coercion and relying solely on reason (including complete mastery of quantitative methods) can figure out and will optimally supply consumers with the quantity and assortment of goods and services that maximize purchasers' utilities at least competitive factor cost. This requires them to competitively maximize profits with full knowledge of ideal technological possibilities, and cost functions (continuous, twice differentiable and monotonic), by producing to the point where marginal revenue equals marginal cost. The behavior is an implication of the Enlightenment notion that reason suffices for consumers to glimpse and achieve the ideal through the actions of the invisible hand and perfect government administration. If these assumptions are satisfied, then it is easily shown that utility-seeking individuals in their roles as consumers and producers in the private and public sectors will achieve the best outcomes not only in the present but also throughout their lifetimes.

There are two versions of idealist neoclassical supply theory: hard and soft. The hard version requires instantaneous acquisition, processing, and application of complete and accurate information about everything that effects supply (see Appendix 3 for a mathematical proof from the standpoint of multiproduct firms). The premise is obviously untenable and can only be employed for didactic purposes. The soft version relaxes the premise by requiring decision makers to profit maximize and cost minimize as best as they can within the possibilities of real time data acquisition, processing, and application. This greatly reduces scale of profit maximizing and cost minimizing, making it seem as if suppliers are primarily optimizers.

The problem with the soft version of neoclassical supply, however, is that the information at hand may be insufficient to profit maximize and cost minimize even after taking account of stochastic factors. This is the realist position. Advocates of bounded rationality contend that many suppliers confronted with sundry imponderables involving production and cost functions, intermediate input availabilities and costs, and product demand, substitute other decision rules for profit maximization and cost minimization. Realists claim that bounded rationality transforms erstwhile optimizing suppliers into satisficers, who sub-optimize where they can, but rely primarily on heuristic methods otherwise instead of profit maximization and cost minimizing. Satisficers seek to better themselves as Enlightenment idealism requires, but bounded rationality inclines them to be contented with "good enough," without exhaustively investigating potentially missed opportunities. Producers like consumers operate under the principles of local non-satiation, sub-optimizing where they can, and employing heuristic methods otherwise.

Vulnerable Assumptions

It is important to appreciate from the outset that idealist neoclassical supply theory cannot be treated separately from consumer behavior. The scope of consumer rationality can be assessed based solely on available supplies, but the neoclassical concept of consumer sovereignty obligates suppliers to produce and distribute goods with appropriate characteristics in accordance with market demand. This means that the validity of the soft idealist version of neoclassical optimization theory depends on all the vulnerable assumptions elaborated in Chapter 4, plus a complementary set of premises strictly pertinent to supply. The number of vulnerable axioms increases from 8 to 17. For the readers' convenience, the neoclassical theory's dubious consumer demand assumptions are restated below together with the additional supply side assumptions essential for assuring soft neoclassical theory's validity. They are:

1) **Consumers possess well-defined continuous preferences,**
2) **Consumer preferences are interpersonally independent,**

3) **Consumers rationally select,**
4) **Consumers exhaustively utility search** (optimizing rather than satisficing),
5) **Consumers autonomously choose** (individuals and households),
6) **Consumers act ethically (competitively)** within the framework of a Lockean social contract,
7) **Well-being is solely determined by successive rational marginal choices.**
8) **Consumer preferences are formed rationally,**
9) **Production and cost functions are continuous, twice differentiable and monotonic,**
10) **Suppliers have complete knowledge of demand and intermediate input acquisition possibilities,**
11) **Suppliers possess well-defined continuous preferences that enable them to optimize with discrete production and cost functions, as well as restricted information on intermediate input supplies and demand,**
12) **Supplier (manager) preferences are interpersonally independent,**
13) **Managers rationally select,**
14) **Managers exhaustively search profit and cost minimization possibilities** (optimizing rather than satisficing),
15) **Managers autonomously choose** (CEOs and collective corporate decision makers),
16) **Managers act ethically (competitively)** within the framework of a Lockean social contract,
17) **Managers' preferences are formed rationally.**

It should be self-evident after careful scrutinizing axioms 9–17 that both hard and soft versions of idealist neoclassical supply theory are untenable. Many production and cost functions are not continuous, twice differentiable, and monotonic. Suppliers do not have complete knowledge of demand and intermediate input acquisition possibilities. They do not possess well-defined continuous preferences to deal with lapses that arise in axioms 9 and 10. Suppliers do not possess well-defined continuous preferences that enable them to optimize with discrete production and cost functions, as well as restricted information on intermediate input supplies and demand. Supplier (manager) preferences may be interpersonally dependent. Managers may not rationally select. Managers may not exhaustively search profit and cost minimization possibilities (optimizing rather than satisficing). Managers may not autonomously choose (CEOs and collective corporate decision makers). Managers may act unscrupulously (anti-competitively) outside the framework of a Lockean social contract. Managers' preferences may not be rationally formed.

In a nutshell, the soft version of idealist neoclassical supply theory is not good enough. The assumptions are partly or wholly counterfactual making it unreasonable to accept the claim that suppliers profit maximize and cost minimize. Managers are neither ideally efficient, nor incorruptible, and therefore may well operate on neo-realist ideocratic basis (see Part II).

This is where realists come into the supply side picture. Advocates of bounded rationality, accepting the evidence that suppliers (managers) do not optimize, have sought to discover the precise motives (heuristics) governing production, and to assess whether divergences are mild enough to support the conclusion that market processes are broadly utility enhancing and beneficial. Neoclassical realism thus is distinguished from soft neoclassical idealism by the importance it places on how suppliers actually behave rather than on whether market systems facilitate efficiency and adhere sufficiently to Smithian and Lockean ethics. The same principles apply to soft idealist and realist neoclassical perceptions of government efficiency and ethics.

Although, no complete bounded rational theory of economics exists, neoclassical or otherwise,[1] this chapter provides some examples of realist neoclassical supply theory revealing precisely how managerial choice may

---

[1] Reinhard Selten (2002). "What is Bounded Rationality?," in Gigerenzer, Gerd and Selten, Reinhard (eds.), *Bounded Rationality The Adaptive Toolbox*, Cambridge, MA: MIT Press. Selten has pointed out, "A comprehensive, coherent theory of bounded rationality is not available. This is a task for the future." We do not have a theory whose axiomatic basis enables us to deduce implications of the theory in mathematical form. Simon described human reasoning as follows: We know today that human reasoning, the product of bound rationality, can be characterized as selective search through large spaces of possibilities. The selectivity of the search, hence its feasibility, is obtained by applying rules of thumb, or heuristics, to determine what paths should be traced and what ones can be ignored. The search halts when a satisfactory solution has been found, almost always long before all alternatives have been examined (Simon, 1992, p. 3).

significantly depart from ideal requirements. It shows that in many cases, firms move toward a satisficing space and once they operate in the attractor or satisficing space, they will continue to do so until conditions change. This is the supply-side satisficing counterpart to consumer-side "local nonsatiation," and means that no equilibrium, unique or otherwise, can be deduced for any competitive groups or for their members, precluding hard version idealist neoclassical outcomes.

Attractors, Bounded Rationality, and Creative Destruction

To appreciate why this is the case, let us consider the choice problem between maximizing sales and profits posed by William Baumol in a bounded rational universe that precludes ideal optimization of both the perfectly and transitorily imperfectly competitive types.[2] Baumol, on the basis of his consultant experience concluded that "optimizing" businessmen (firm managers) were more interested in maximizing sales than profits once an acceptable level of profit had been attained, prompting him to infer that they wanted to maximize revenue subject to a profit constraint. Since this also requires knowledge of product and factor demand equations, it cannot be done ideally, but it is possible for a firm by lowering price to increase revenue and thus perhaps increase market share.[3]

---

[2]William Baumol (1959). *Business Behavior, Value and Growth* (rev. ed), New York: Macmillan.

[3]There are at least three definitions of market share–profit share, output share, and revenue share. Maximizing profits is consistent with maximizing profit share, so no conflict between firm behavior and the assumption of profit–maximization arises. Output share is subject to an "apples and oranges" problem because the products of different firms may be heterogeneous with regards to design and, as perceived by buyers, quality. Therefore, in the formal model, it is assumed that market share is measured as the share of industry revenues. First, it sometimes happens that the volume of future sales depends on prior achieved levels. For example, the sale of razor blades often depends on the number of razors and therefore razor blades in use. Similarly, adopting Word instead of WordPerfect should be preferable because Word's large market share allows users' greater scope for document sharing. Second, increasing market share may discourage would-be competitors. If it appears that entrants might face stiff competition from dominant firms, prospective new entrants may decide that discretion is the better part of valor. Third, managers may succumb to moral hazard placing their private interest above firm owners'. Managers are not "residual claimants" and therefore may be more interested in market share than profits because this usually increases their compensation. (See Adolf Berle and Gardner Means (1932). *The Modern Corporation and*

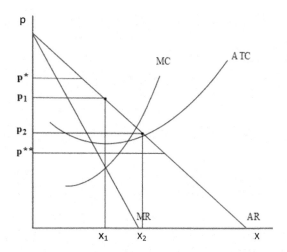

Figure 5.1   Feasible Monopolistic Production.

Consider a limited plane space denoted by Γ and a subspace within Γ denoted by Ω. We also consider a type of motion that takes place within Γ. If motion of this type starts within Γ but not within Ω and always ends within Ω, then Ω is an attractor. We will return to this definition after developing an example devised by Edward Beltrami.[4]

Figure 5.1 depicts the non-ideal (and imperfectly competitive) consumer product demand and producer factor cost curves of a monopolistic firm. It can be estimated, but for practical and econometric reasons, the monopolistic firm knows that it is unreliable. Ideal demand curves as explained in Chapter 4 do not exist.

p_1 and p_2 are the implied (but non-determinable) ideal (or short-run imperfectly competitive ideal) profit maximizing and revenue maximizing prices respectively. Suppose the firm, unable to locate p_1 and p_2 set the price p^* above the profit maximizing price. The management may find that this price is too high when evaluated from the standpoint of bounded rational product demand and factor supply curves because the quantity sold is small

---

Private Property, New York: Macmillan.) Fourth, large market share sometimes makes it easier to raise capital on private equity markets because investors equate size with success, or anticipate that lending to this type of firm will make it an attractive takeover candidate.
[4]Edward Beltrami (1987). *Mathematics for Dynamic Modeling*, Boston: Academic Press, p. 208.

and profits are not as large as expected. They may decide to lower the price to a small amount. This will set a price nearer the bounded rational profit maximizing and the revenue maximizing price. Clearly, this is a desirable result since both profit and revenue are larger.

The success invites repetition that will continue until a price lower than p_1 but larger than p_2 is fixed. A further reduction will reduce profit and increase revenue. A price decrease no longer increases both. The firm is in its attractor.

If the firm had started with a price of p^{**}, price increases would raise both profit and revenue until the price had been raised above p_2. If the price is greater than or equal to p_2 and less than or equal to p_1, the firm is in the attractor.

It will set a price at or below the profit maximizing price and at or above the revenue maximizing price. In other words, it will operate at one of the maximizing prices or at a price between them. If it sets prices outside this price interval, it can increase both profit and revenue by moving toward the interval. This closed interval from p_1 to p_2 inclusive is the firm's attractor. The firm will always seek to be operative within its attractor.

This example meets the definition of an attractor given above. The space Γ is the demand curve between intersections with the axis or other extreme points. The type of motion is changing the production level and the attractor, corresponding to Ω is the demand curve from and including p_1 to p_2.

Why should a monopoly care about revenue and satisficing? Should not it care only about profit? Not necessarily because satisficing discourages potential competition.

Although the firm does not know the precise location of either the ideal or the bounded rational demand curve, it can find out when it is in the attractor by varying its price. If profit and revenue change in the same direction, it is not in the attractor. If they change in opposite directions or if one objective does not change, they are in the attractor. These points may easily be verified by reference to Figure 5.1.

If the firm is in its attractor and lowers its price, with the lower price also within the attractor, it will increase revenue and lose profit. Revenue will increase because bounded rational demand is elastic (marginal revenue is positive) in the attractors. Profit will decline to the right of the profit maximizing marginal cost because margin cost in this region is greater than marginal revenue.

On the other hand, if the firm when it is in the attractor raises its price, the new price also being in the attractor, revenue will decline and profit will increase. Revenue will decline with the higher price because demand is elastic. Profit will increase because selling fewer units lowers cost, and since marginal cost is greater than marginal revenue, profit will increase. These points may be verified by reference to Figure 5.1.

The behavioral rules of thumb here are straightforward. If a price change causes both profit and revenue to increase, firms should change price again in the same direction. If a price change causes both profit and revenue to decrease, firms should change price in the opposite direction. If a price change results in either profit or revenue increasing while the other decreases, the firm in the attractor must decide which goal is best. If either profit or revenue remains the same and the other one increases, the firm is at or near the maximum point for the unchanged objective. Again a decision is required.

Suppose that the monopolist's worst fear is realized and a competing firm enters the market. This alters the original firm's estimated demand equation and the estimated demand curve will shift each time that the competitor changes its price. Thus, the attractor changes with the competitors' price changes. But the attractor still remains attractive. Following its self-interest will still lead the firm toward and into the new attractor. In short, satisficing supply side theory shows that monopolistic firms (and competitive ones too) can behave diversely in what seems to be ideally rational ways without nudging the state of the system toward ideal competitive or imperfectly competitive equilibrium. It could be true that each firm may believe that it is optimizing, but Baumol fails to adequately appreciate that this cannot be so for the ideal system in its entirety. Suppliers under this sort of regime are responsive to bounded rational consumer demand, and do not have any ideally reliable way of choosing between profit and market share maximizing.[5]

---

[5]The same problem held in a more extreme form in Soviet enterprises. See Steven Rosefielde (2007). *Russian Economy from Lenin to Putin*, New York: Wiley.

Firm Revenue and Profit in a Competing Group

Let us now consider the general case of rival firms (see Appendix 4 for more complex cases of interdependent variables). Assume that the number of firms is small enough so that each firm can affect the market by changing its price, but there is more than one firm. A bounded rational product demand equation exists for each firm but no firm knows it with precision. The same principle holds for primary and intermediate factor supply curves behind the scenes.

A product demand equation for each of the n firms in the competing group can be formulated as:

$$x_i = f_i(p_1, \ldots, p_n, m), \quad \forall_{i=1}^n,$$

where x_i is the quantity sold by the ith firm, the p's indicate the prices charged by the firms and m indicates the income of the buyers. We also specify that $\frac{\partial x_i}{\partial p_i} < 0$, $\frac{\partial x_i}{\partial p_i} > 0$, $j \neq$ i, and $\frac{\partial x_i}{\partial m} > 0$. Because buyer's income is exogenous to the market and we are interested in interactions within the market, we will ignore income terms.

Each firm is interested in revenue because it contributes to profits and market share. Revenue for firm i is

$$R_i = p_i x_i.$$

Firms that are interested in gaining market share will try to increase revenue by lowering their prices. The change can be shown as:[6]

$$dR_i = x_i dp_i + p_i \frac{\partial x_i}{\partial p_i} dp_i + \sum_{k \neq i} \frac{\partial x_i}{\partial p_k} dp_k. \tag{5.1}$$

---

[6]Many of the relationships that will be developed could be stated in elasticity terms. For example, if $dp_i < 0$ and $dR_i > 0$, then using (5.1) we can easily obtain

$$(1 + \epsilon_{ii}) \frac{dp_i}{p_i} \sum_{k \neq i} \epsilon_{ik} \frac{dp_k}{p_k}.$$

Here, ϵ_{ii} is good i's own price elasticity coefficient and ϵ_{ik} is the cross elasticity of i with respect to the price of good k. It seems more straightforward to use price and quantities rather than elasticity coefficients.

Income terms are ignored because we assume that demand is elastic for small competitive firms. Note that if price is reduced by firm i, the first term on the right will be negative but the second term will be positive. The second will be larger in absolute amount if and only if the firm is operating at a point at which its demand is elastic in its attractor.

The summation in (5.1), the third term on the right, shows the effect on firm i's revenue of price changes by competing firms. Clearly, this summation must be considered when the firm is trying to anticipate the effects of its own price change. If the firm lowers its price to increase revenue or increases its price to increase profit, the summation of the effects of other firms' price changes may offset its effort in whole or in part. Of course, since the firm does not know its demand equation, it does not know the mathematical statement of the summation but it will know that the forces represented by the summation are operating even though it cannot measure their effects.

During our presentation and discussion of the attractor, we assume that if the firms are in their attractors and if $dp_i < 0$, then $dR_i > 0$; i.e., that other firms' price changes effect the firm's revenue but do not offset completely the effect of the firm's own price change on its own revenue when firm i is in its attractor. This permits the firm to set prices with the direction of the result being the same in the absence of competitors. Of course, the magnitude of change will vary with competitors' actions, but the direction will not. In Appendix 3, the effects of price changes on competitors' revenues are discussed. It will also be argued that $dp_j < 0$ implies $dR_i > 0$ will often be empirically accurate.

To deal with profit, we introduce cost. The total cost for firm is shown by

$$k_i = k_i(x_i, w_1, \ldots, w_q).$$

While incremental cost is

$$dK_i = \frac{\partial K_i}{\partial x_i} \frac{\partial x_i}{\partial p_i} dp_i + \frac{\partial K_i}{\partial x_i} \sum_{k \neq i} \frac{\partial x_i}{\partial p_k} dp_k. \tag{5.2}$$

The w's being the prices of factors of production, which we assume to be constant throughout our discussion. Also $\frac{\partial K_i}{\partial x_i} > 0$. Profit can now be written as

$$\pi_i = p_i f_i(p_1, \ldots, p_n, m) - K_i(x_i, w_1, \ldots, w_q).$$

Ignoring income effects as before, we write the profit differential as

$$dπ_i = x_i dp_i + p_i \frac{\partial x_i}{\partial p_i} dp_i + p_i \sum_{k \neq i} \frac{\partial x_i}{\partial p_k} dp_k$$

$$- \frac{\partial K_i}{\partial x_i} \frac{\partial x_i}{\partial p_i} dp_i - \frac{\partial K_i}{\partial x_i} \sum_{k \neq i} \frac{\partial x_i}{\partial p_k} dp_k \qquad (5.3)$$

$$dR_i - dK_i,$$

or as

$$dπ_i = x_i dp_i + \left(p_i - \frac{\partial k_i}{\partial x_i} \right) \frac{\partial x_i}{\partial p_i} dp_i + \left(p_i - \frac{\partial k_i}{\partial x_i} \right) \sum_{k \neq i} \frac{\partial x_i}{\partial p_k} dp_k. \qquad (5.4)$$

The effects of competitor's price changes on profits also must be considered. Just as we assumed in the revenue case that $dp_i < 0$ implies $dR_i > 0$, we assume likewise that $dp_i > 0$ implies $dπ_i > 0$. The assumption is examined in Appendix 4. It will be argued that the assumption often will be valid.

The Attractor[7]

As in the simple monopoly case, the attractor is the range of product prices and values bounded by the profit maximizing price and the revenue maximizing price.

Let $\bar{p}_1$ be the profit maximizing price, then according to (5.3), this is the price at which $dR_i = dK_i$. Since this is the profit maximizing point, at a price higher than $\bar{p}_1$, $dR_i > dK_i$. Thus, if the firm lowers its price

---

[7]The attractors that we derive are not "strange attractors." The latter require the presence of a fractal and sensitivity to initial conditions. Our attractors do not meet either of these requirements.

but still has a price higher than $\bar{p}_1$, it increases revenue and profit. At a price lower than $\bar{p}_1$ but still in the attractor, we have $dR_i < dK_i$. Thus, revenue has increased because price is lower but cost has increased even more. Consequently, profit is reduced.

As price is lowered from $\bar{p}_1$, revenue will increase by smaller and smaller amounts until $dR_i = 0$, which locates the price, call it $\hat{p}_1$ at which revenue is maximized.

Thus, we have $\bar{p}_1$ the highest point of firm i's attractor and $\hat{p}_1$, the lowest. For points outside the attractor, prices higher than $\bar{p}_1$ or lower than $\hat{p}_i$, a price move toward the attractor increases both revenue and profit. Such a move generates $d\pi_i dR_i > 0$.

Within the attractor, i.e., at prices between $\bar{p}_1$ and $\hat{p}_1$ inclusive, a price decline increases revenue and increases cost more than revenue, thus lowering profit. For a price increase within the attractor, revenue decreases but cost decreases even more thus increasing profit. Hence for either a price increase or decrease in the attractor, $d\pi_i dR_i \leq 0$.

The heuristics are the same as in the monopoly case. The question of whether all firms can be in their attractors at the same time is critical because satisficing theory depends on all firms seeking their attractors and remaining in them. It is analogous to the general equilibrium question: Can all firms optimize simultaneously? The issue for bounded rationality is whether all firms can reach satisfactory levels simultaneously.

To answer the question, recall that in a firm's attractor, incremental cost and incremental revenue are equal only at the profit maximizing point, the attractor's highest point. At all other points in the attractor, incremental cost is positive and larger than incremental revenue.

In turn, incremental revenue is positive at all except the lowest point of the attractor where the value is zero. This last point is the revenue maximizing point.

Consequently, the attractor can be described by the following statements:

$$dK_i > 0$$

$$dR_i \geq 0$$

$$dK_i - dR_i \geq 0, \quad \forall_{i=1}^{n}. \tag{5.5}$$

Production and Costs 73

The first two inequalities assure that the equality in (5.5) will hold only when $dK_i = dR_i$, i.e., only at the profit maximizing point, the highest point in the attractor. At other points, $dK_i > dR_i$.

The second inequality requires that $dR_i = 0$ only at the revenue maximum. This is the lowest point in the attractor. Beyond this point, at lower prices, $dR_i < 0$.

Thus, we have a description of the attractor in the inequalities written above. The only remaining question is whether (5.5) can hold for all firms at the same time. To answer this question, we need to examine the inequalities,

$$dK_i - dR_i = \frac{\partial K_i}{\partial x_i}\frac{\partial x_i}{\partial p_i}dp_i + \frac{\partial K_i}{\partial x_i}\sum_{k\neq i}\frac{\partial x_i}{\partial p_k}dp_k$$

$$- x_i dp_i - p_i\frac{\partial x_i}{\partial p_i}dp_i - p_i\sum_{k\neq i}\frac{\partial x_i}{\partial p_k}dp_k \geq 0, \quad \forall_{i=1}^n.$$

We simplify the notation:

$$a_{ii} = \frac{\partial K_i}{\partial x_i}\frac{\partial x_i}{\partial p_i} - x_i - p_i\frac{\partial x_i}{\partial p_i},$$

$$a_{ij} = \frac{\partial K_i}{\partial x_i}\frac{\partial x_i}{\partial p_j} - p_i\frac{\partial x_i}{\partial p_j},$$

and form the matrix

$$A = \begin{bmatrix} a_{11} & \cdots & a_{1n} \\ \vdots & \ddots & \vdots \\ a_{n1} & \cdots & a_{nn} \end{bmatrix},$$

which we will argue is non-singular.

Now the inequality in (5.5) can be shown as

$$\begin{bmatrix} a_{11} & \cdots & a_{1n} \\ \vdots & \ddots & \vdots \\ a_{n1} & \cdots & a_{nn} \end{bmatrix}\begin{bmatrix} dp_1 \\ \vdots \\ dp_n \end{bmatrix} \geq 0$$

or as

$$Adp \geq 0, \qquad\qquad (5.6)$$

0 being the zero column vector.

To parse the subject further, we rewrite (5.5) as

$$Adp = \alpha. \qquad\qquad (5.7)$$

Here, α is a vector whose elements are either zeros or positive numbers. This is true because they are the differences between incremental cost and incremental revenue, in other words, they satisfy (5.5) and consequently they cannot be negative. Each row in A represents the dK_i, dR_i for each company; that is, each competitor is represented by a row in A. Since the competitors do not know their demand equations, they cannot maximize profit exactly. Therefore, a zero will appear in α only when the firm has stumbled on the precise maximization of profit. Otherwise, the elements of α are the positive differences between incremental cost and incremental revenue and (5.5) shows they will be positive. Even though they may not think of it this way, every firm wants to be in its attractor. This is true simply because they can increase both profit and revenue by moving into their attractor. But what do they do, once they are there?

A firm could increase price in an attempt to increase or even maximize profit. If profit is already judged to be satisfactory, this is likely to be unattractive because it involves shooting in the dark. That is the firm does not know its demand equation and it may not know how competitors will respond. Thus, it faces two kinds of uncertainty about the outcome which makes price increases unattractive if profit is at an acceptable level.

If profit is judged to be meager, a price increase might be considered especially if the firm's price appears low in comparison to competitors. But this also involves shooting in the dark and carries with it a loss of revenue and perhaps market share. Price increases are likely to be undertaken with caution.

It is not unusual for the senior executives of a company to speak publically about their uncertainty about whether they should raise price and thus increase profit, or lower price to increase market share. In each case they are contemplating, the anticipated outcomes are in their attractors.

The firm could consider a price decrease to bolster market share. This however is shooting in the dark and risks a price war. Price competition and price changes generally therefore are likely to be undertaken with caution, except in special types of markets.

Advertising may offer an alternative to price competition. Unfortunately, it is often futile because competitors respond in kind, even though firms may feel compelled to advertise for defensive reasons. Curtailing or shunning advertising may appreciably reduce sales.

Price changes and advertising are short-run moves and consequently are limited in their ability to change the attractors of the firms even though each firm may want to change its own and its competitors' attractor to win at its rivals' expense. Price changes will not do this and advertising is unlikely to be predictably more effective.

Creative Destruction

Is there a third way? Can competitive firms change cost and demand equations by other means? There are several alternatives: developing new or improved products, generating more efficient methods of production, finding new markets, or devising new forms of industrial organization. Two things stand out about these: they are long-run processes and reminiscent of Joseph Schumpeter's dynamic theory of capitalist economic development.[8]

Schumpeter described capitalism as an "evolutionary process" primarily driven by new consumer goods, markets, productive techniques, transportation and communication systems, and innovative forms of industrial organization. War, revolution, cataclysmic events, population growth, and monetary policy were secondary. The driver is competitive intra-market innovation and modernization. It creates new and destroys old economic structures. "This process of Creative Destruction is the essential fact about capitalism. It is what capitalism consists of and what every capitalist concern has got to live in."[9]

---

[8]Joseph Schumpeter (1942). *Capitalism, Socialism and Democracy*, New York: Harper and Row, p. 82 *et seq.*
[9]*Ibid.*, p. 83.

Short-run operations of course remain competitively important, but it is primarily creative destruction that generates new attractors. Richard D'Aveni's empirical research on innovation and modernization (creative destruction) confirms this claim.[10]

Conclusion

We have crafted a realist description of monopolistic and competitive firm behavior in the short and long run in case of a group of single product firms, where satisficing displaces optimization in whole or part using three concepts: bounded rationality, attractors, and creative destruction. Similar principles apply to retailing (see Appendix 5). Bounded rationality and attractors jointly form a short-run model that is compatible with Schumpeter's dynamic.[11] It proves that all documented economic behavior ascribed or ascribable to ideal competitive utility and profit maximization can be replicated with satisficing theory without making untenable assumptions. This means not only that ideal and short-run imperfectly competitive theories are superfluous, but that they are also necessarily exaggerate and distort real accomplishments. No serious economist can deny this inference, but many tend to brush the insight aside by supposing that exaggerations and distortions are slight because "normal" economies are "workably" competitive. Outcomes may not be ideal, but they are nearly as good as they can humanly be.

This counterargument is specious. The deep problem is that consumers, workers, investors, financiers, suppliers and government regulators have weakly defined and ill-informed preference functions, a fragile understanding of opportunity costs and key players operate with mixed motives. Material outcomes and well-being therefore significantly deviate from both

---

[10]Richard D'Aveni (1994). *Hypercompetition: Managing the Dynamics of Strategic Maneuvering*, New York: Free Press.

[11]Schumpeter suggested that creative destruction was a process beyond the perimeters of optimization theory, but this is so only on a very narrow interpretation of ideal optimization. He wrote: "A system — any system economic or other — that at every given point of time fully utilizes its possibilities to the best advantage may yet in the long run be inferior to a system that does so at no given point of time, because the latter's failure to do so may be a condition for the level or speed of long run performance." p. 83.

the workably competitive and ideal standards. The magnitudes cannot be finely calibrated using idealistic rules of thumb and must be evaluated case by case to assess losses and devise appropriate regulatory interventions. The alternative is grasping at straws.[12]

[12]Frédéric Laville (2000). "Should We Abandon Optimization Theory? The Need for Bounded Rationality," *The Journal of Economic Methodology*, Vol. 7, pp. 422–423. Laville summarizes the case against optimization theory as follows: (1) Empirical evidence has confounded optimization theory; in the face of experimental studies, an empirical dilemma has emerged, according to which we should discard either expected utility (EU) theory or the criterion of empirical refutation. (2) Methodological criticisms have attacked optimization theory's epistemological status; together, they give rise to a methodological dilemma, according to which optimization theory is indeterminate, un-falsifiable or tautological. (3) Methodological defenses appeared to protect optimization theory against criticism; but a more careful examination has shown that either they involved logical defects, or they rest upon a conceptual gap. (4) Theoretical difficulties have plagued optimal theory; though various extensions have been proposed, optimization theory entails a theoretical dilemma, according to which one must choose between unrealistic environment and unrealistic abilities.

Chapter 6

Institutions

The Philosophes believed that reason would lead mankind to design and adopt institutions required for optimally functioning, self-regulating neoclassical economic systems. These institutions were supposed to be pro-competitive and consistent with John Locke's social contract. They include private property protections and civil rights. Whatever the specifics turned out to be, they had to satisfy these criteria, and in this sense were "constitutional" as distinct from "legislative" regulations.

The Philosophes' faith that free men and women would discover how to construct ideal and workable founding institutions constitutes yet another vulnerable neoclassical axiom, the 18th. It stipulates that humans can either directly intuit ideal founding institutions, or can learn how to do so by trial and error. The idealist version disregards the concept of bounded rationality; the realist version embraces it. The first contends that the search for founding institutions will be good enough for all economic actors to optimize; the second accepts the logic of beneficial utility-searching, but settles for satisficing. In the realist world people rely on heuristic methods to utility search and don't primarily profit maximize and cost minimize in the full competitive sense.

The idealist case for optimization is self-evidently invalidated by the vulnerabilities of the first 17 axioms. Individuals and collectives cannot know enough to universally optimize without resort to heuristic methods, so that it follows directly that they cannot devise founding institutions that make the impossible possible. Satisficing is neoclassical theory's only hope. Perhaps, a set of founding institutions can be created that does the

79

trick and is sustainable. Many claim that the American constitution fills the bill, but this overlooks the fact that the powers wielded by the Federal government today are vastly greater than in 1789, and hamstring the free market.[1]

Apparently, imagining ideal neoclassical founding institutions is easier said than done. The European Union postwar effort to solve this problem provides insight into the magnitude of the challenge.

Postwar European leaders blamed war on nationalism and resolved to solve the problem by devising a trans-European constitution compatible with neoclassical theory (social democratic variant) that transferred responsibility for many fundamental aspects of national government from individual European countries to higher transnational bodies, creating a two tiered system.[2] They formed the European Union (EU) as a political entity to implement this "supranational" dream,[3] and created seven high tier sub-institutions to perform the delegated tasks: the European Parliament, Council of the European Union, European Commission, the European Council, ECB, Court of Justice of the European Union and European Court of Auditors.[4]

---

[1] Steven Rosefielde and Quinn Mills (2014). *Democracy and its Elected Enemies*, Cambridge: Cambridge University Press. Thomas Mann and Norman Ornstein (2013). *It's Even Worse Than It Looks: How the American Constitutional System Collided With the New Politics of Extremism*, New York: Basic Books.

[2] Yun Chen and Ken Morita (2012). *"Toward an East Asian Community,"* in Steven Rosefielde, Masaaki Kuboniwa and Satoshi Mizobata, (eds.), *Prevention and Crisis Management: Lessons for Asia from the 2008 Crisis*, Singapore: World Scientific.

[3] There are 17 members of the Eurozone: Austria, Belgium, Cyprus, Estonia, Finland, France, Germany, Greece, Ireland, Italy, Luxembourg, Malta, Netherlands, Portugal, Slovakia, Slovenia, and Spain. It is officially called the euro area, and is an economic and monetary union (EMU). Other EU states are obliged to join once they qualify, except the United Kingdom and Denmark. Members cannot secede or be expelled in principle. Monetary policy is the responsibility of the European Central Bank (ECB). Monaco, San Marino and Vatican City have concluded formal agreements with the EU to use the euro. Andorra will do so July 1, 2013. Kosovo and Montenegro have unilaterally adopted the euro, but are not EU members.

[4] Wolfram Kaiser and Peter Starie (eds.) (2009). *Transnational European Union: Towards a Common Political Space*, London: Routledge. Richard Baldwin and Charles Wyplosz (2012). *The Economics of European Integration*, 4th edn., New York: McGraw Hill.

These supranational bodies were granted exclusive competence over: (1) the "customs union," (2) competition policy, (3) eurozone (EZ) monetary power, (4) a common fisheries policy, (5) a common commercial policy, (6) conclusion of certain international agreements.

They were also given the right to shared competence in (7) the internal market, (8) social policy for aspects defined in the treaty, (9) agriculture and fisheries, excluding the conservation of marine biological resources, (10) environment, (11) consumer protection, (12) transport, (13) trans-European networks, (14) energy, (15) the area of freedom, security and justice, (16) common safety concerns in public health aspects defined in the treaty, (17) research, development, technology and space, (18) development, cooperation and humanitarian aid, (19) coordination of economic and social policies, (20) common security and defense policies.

Additionally, supranational bodies enjoy supporting competence in (21) protection and improvement of human health, (22) industry, (23) culture, (24) tourism, (25) education, youth sport and vocational training, (26) civil protection (disaster prevention), and (27) administration.

This list makes it plain that supranationality is an administrative scheme intended more to control consumer choice and manage business than a constitution designed to empower efficient bounded rational regulated consumer utility satisficing, and business profit maximizing and cost minimizing. There are pro-competitive aspects, but no recognition of the need for efficient bounded rational governance. The endeavor is a bureaucratic project that assigns administrative jurisdictions; not the establishment of Enlightenment regimes that place reason in command. Neoclassical consumer utility seeking, profit seeking and cost consciousness are channeled by "sovereign" bureaucratic dictate, without any serious effort to maximize social welfare under prevailing bounded rational constraints.

It is possible to devise theories of perfect governance that reconcile the Enlightenment and social democratic visions within the complete neoclassical paradigm,[5] but as will be discussed in Chapter 8 practice is entirely divorced from the principles of optimal publicly regulated competitive

[5]James Meade (1993). *Liberty, Equality and Efficiency*, New York: New York University Press.

control. If EU leaders actually harbored such lofty aspirations, the aftermath of the 2008 financial crisis proves that they failed.[6]

Further insight into the axiomatic flaws of EU supranationality has already been provided in Chapter 4. The EU is afflicted with a two tiered quarrelsome family problem. Its supranational leaders don't possess a unitary preference function with completely defined continuous and discrete preferences over an unrestricted domain, and national authorities have conflicting interests.[7]

Under this scheme the European Council acts as paterfamilias over six exclusive administrative preserves, shares responsibility in 14 areas, and accepts the sovereignty of national paterfamilias over un-enumerated rights including taxation and fiscal policy. The arrangement encourages double gaming.

Policies under the sovereign jurisdiction of members should be consistent with those of transnational authorities so that consent at the collective supranational tier is not subverted by dissent at the national tier. Specifically, in the case of the EZ, macroeconomic stability requires that national fiscal policies must be accommodated to transnational monetary policy to achieve best results. Individual members shouldn't overspend because spillover effects diminish the national utility of others. Just as family spendthrifts without malice of forethought often cause damage by inadvertently shifting adjustment costs within households, EZ big deficit spenders harm the entire supranational community by disregarding the monetary consensus (in reality ECB dictate).

---

[6] Steven Rosefielde and Assaf Razin (2012). "A Tale of a Politically-Failing Single-Currency Area," *Israel Economic Review*, Vol. 10, No. 1, pp. 125–138. Rosefielde and Assaf Razin (December, 2012). "What Really Ails the Eurozone?: Faulty Supranational Architecture," *Contemporary Economics*, Vol. 6, No. 4, pp. 10–18. Steven Rosefielde, "Secular Crisis: The Mundell-FlemingTrilemma and EU De-Legitimation," paper presented at the conference on Economic and Political Crises in Europe and the United States, University of Trento, Trento Italy, November 7–9, 2013. Forthcoming in Bruno Dallago and John McGowan (eds.) (2015), *Economic and Political Crises in Europe and the United States: Prospects of Policy Cooperation*, London: Routledge.

[7] The same household problem holds with the supranational and national leaderships, but is assumed away here for didactic purposes.

This particular satisficing problem is unique to the EZ's supranational institutional architecture fixed by the Maastricht Treaty (1992),[8] insofar as it adds a novel dimension to "family" double-gaming.[9] The rules are simple. Nations voluntarily joining the EZ agreed to (1) surrender independent control over the foreign exchange rate, money supply and key aspects of interest rates, but (2) retained authority to tax, deficit spend, borrow from abroad and partially regulate credit. By analogy this meant that household members vested a family council with authority to issue and discount IOUs, and to set the terms of most borrowing and lending, but dad, mom and the kiddies could still overspend their allowances by obtaining credit from each other, and borrowing from outsiders. The arrangement would not pose problems for the rational utilitarian optimizing model where members suppress their self-interest for the household's collective well being because the family's collective IOUs and member financial programs are assumed to be harmoniously optimal, however in disharmonious realist households prodigal members overspend, leaving the rest of the family to clean up the mess. Little Greek brother Antonis Samaras "needs" to live as lavishly as his big German sister Angela Merkel and is going to do whatever it takes to do it.

EZ nations had good reasons to be wary of Maastricht's supranational Procrustean bed. The EMU was a dubious candidate for an optimal currency area because although it trades intensively within the region, sundry barriers

---

[8]The road to the European monetary unification, the centerpiece of a full European Economic Community and Union, went through the European Monetary System (EMS) 1979–1998, where eight member countries tried to dampen fluctuations in their foreign exchange rate parities. They effectively pegged their currencies to the Deutsche Mark in an effort to curb inflation and advance towards European Monetary integration. The experiment failed. In 1992 important members exited the EMS. Nonetheless, eleven members of the European Union upped the ante by choosing a solution that required more, rather than less cooperation. On January 1, 1999 they created a common currency area (EMU: European Monetary Union) that effectively imposed a fixed exchange rate among all member countries. Participants surrendered their authority over national monetary policy and vested it in the supranational hands of the European Central Bank (ECB), forcing members to rely exclusively on fiscal and regulatory policy to manage macroeconomic disequilibria.

[9]Analogous satisficing behaviors can be observed in unitary states and centralized federations, but the record suggests that supranationality exacerbated already difficult inter-state European Community (EC) economic relationships.

greatly impair intra-European labor mobility,[10] and members repeatedly failed to honor pledges of monetary and fiscal responsibility.[11] But hope supported by idealist optimization theory triumphed over Simon-style realism and the unscrupulous behavior stressed by neo-realism. It was easy for supranational social democratic idealists to perceive the EU and EZ as a risk free golden opportunity offering: (1) economies of market size, scale and scope; (2) foreign currency exchange savings, seignorage and enhanced creditworthiness benefits, (3) elimination of intra-union borders and a cosmopolitan identity.

Europe had the potential for high volume intra-union trade and labor mobility that would reap significant economies of market size, scale and scope.[12] The creation of an EZ also would improve creditworthiness for less developed members, attract foreign investors, and the community's postwar

---

[10]Free movement of labor is one of the four basic freedoms enshrined in the Acquis Communautaire, and EU leaders frequently reiterate their adherence to the principle. However, a task force headed by Walter Nonneman found that despite good intentions substantial, and perhaps increasing barriers to labor mobility remain. There is "pronounced immobility of the European workforce, that despite high unemployment in the local area, is disinclined to resettle in areas with more job opportunities. Less than 0.5% of European workers move to a different region every year. This is very little, compared, for example, with the 2.5% of Americans who take up residence in a different state every year." Nonneman identifies a host of institutional factors that contribute to this outcome. See Walter Nonneman (July 2007). *European Immigration and the Labor Market*, The Transatlantic Task Force on Immigration and Integration, Migration Policy Institute, Bertelsmann Stiftung. http://www.migrationinformation.org/transatlantic2006/ImmigrationEULaborMarket_72507.pdf.

Cf. "Class of 2012: EU Labor Market Largely Immobile As Young Find Themselves Trapped by Language," Associate Press, December 5, 2012.

[11]Many members failed to honor their Maastricht pledges to contain inflation and deficit spending prior to monetary union. Aspirants seeking EMU accession were supposed to hold inflation to no more than 1.5% per annum; to maintain a stable exchange rate with the assistance of the ERM (exchange rate mechanism), to run public sector deficits less than 3% of GDP, with a public debt under 60% of GDP. Many established members and aspirants alike flunked the tests after they joined the EMU, setting a pernicious precedent for future GIIPS (Greece, Italy, Ireland, Portugal and Spain).

[12]See: Robert A. Mundell (September 1961). "A Theory of Optimum Currency Areas," *American Economic Review*, Vol. 51, pp. 657–664; Ronald I. McKinnon (September 1963). "Optimum Currency Areas", *American Economic Review*, Vol. 53, No. 4, pp. 717–725; Kenen, Peter B. (1967). "Toward a Supranational Monetary System," in G. Pontecorvo, R.P. Shay, and A.G. Hart (eds.), *Issues in Banking and Monetary Analysis*, New York: Holt, Reinhart, and Winston.

commitment to peaceful fraternal cooperation appeared to eliminate fiscal dangers.

Supranational skeptics chary of utopian constitutionalism acknowledged these potential benefits, but tempered their enthusiasm particularly with regard to macroeconomic policy cooperation, pointing out that Maastricht rules might complicate some member's management of macroeconomic disequilibria. Milton Friedman observed that nations can deal more deftly with disorders if they have their own currency, allowing them to vary prices and exchange rates, thereby affecting real wages and unit labor costs, but this requires them to accept high costs of doing business across national boundaries due to stochastically fluctuating exchange rates. If they opt for monetary union to reduce high cross border transactions costs, then they may discover that competitiveness can only be regained by accepting painful deflationary adjustments (reduced Euro denominated prices and wages).

Consequently the volume of intra-regional trade and labor mobility must be very high, and EZ fiscal assistance promises credible to make monetary unions attractive to vulnerable members, while strong prospective EZ members should carefully weigh the potential derivative costs to them of other members' misbehavior.[13]

The adoption of the Euro lured many weak members to intensify current account deficits, diminished their competitiveness and plunged them into extreme indebtedness, which in conjunction with the 2008 global financial crisis sent them into deep depressions from which they have yet to extricate themselves. There is a broad consensus that the Maastricht regime bears substantial blame, but many continue to claim on social democratic idealist grounds that this is a temporary aberration because the EU's

---

[13]Peter Kenen (1967). "Toward a Supranational Monetary System," in G. Pontecorvo, R.P. Shay, and A.G. Hart (eds.), *Issues in Banking and Monetary Analysis*, New York: Holt, Reinhart, and Winston; Paul De Grauwe (March 11, 2010), The Greek Crisis and the Future of the Eurozone Eurointelligence. The structural problem in the Eurozone is created by the fact that the monetary union is not embedded in a political union. See also Paul De Grauwe (2000). *Economics of Monetary Union*, New York: Oxford University Press. Paul De Grauwe (August 19, 2011). "The ECB as a Lender of Last Resort," Marvin Goodfriend (2011). "Central Banking in the Credit Turmoil: An Assessment of Federal Reserve Practice," *Journal of Monetary Economics*.

supranational architecture can be repaired with better fiscal coordination.[14] Their contention is validly deduced from rational utilitarian premises; however, this doesn't settle matters in bounded rational realist and neo-realist world where there are no grounds for supposing that dysfunctional families will ultimately see the light. EU members are apt to remain quarrelsome under various regimes, but even more so when sovereignty is divided between transnational and national entities.[15]

---

[14]Christopher Sims (2012). "Gaps in the Institutional Structure of the Euro Area," *Public Debt, Monetary Policy and Financial Stability*. Thomas Sargent (February, 2012). "Nobel Lecture: United States Then, Europe Now," *Journal of Political Economy*, Vol. 120, No. 1, pp. 1–40.

[15]For a more exhaustive analysis see Steven Rosefielde, "Secular Crisis: The Mundell-FlemingTrilemma and EU De-Legitimation," paper presented at the conference on Economic and Political Crises in Europe and the United States, University of Trento, Trento Italy, November 7–9, 2013. Forthcoming in Bruno Dallago and John McGowan (eds.) (2015) *Economic and Political Crises in Europe and the United States: Prospects of Policy Cooperation*, London: Routledge.

Chapter 7

Macroeconomics

Rational utilitarians from the late 18th century until the publication of John Maynard Keynes's path breaking treatise on *The General Theory of Employment, Interest and Money* took the position that economics understood as comprehensively rational utility-seeking was universal and would necessarily generate best ideal outcomes under prevailing natural constraints both in the short and long runs.[1] Idealist theory required everyone to optimize in the present, and across all their futures. Irving Fisher showed precisely how this should be accomplished in his widely acclaimed treatise on *The Theory of Interest* through a process of "trading with the future" which assured that individual life time utility was not only maximized, but also optimized at every moment from cradle to the grave.[2]

From the rational idealist standpoint anyone interested in assessing aggregate outcomes [Gross domestic product (GDP) and gross national income (GNI)] could compute pertinent statistics by summing across national populations. The "macro" picture assembled in this way however is merely a photographic "blow up" of underlying "micro" realities. It doesn't introduce novel behavioral principles.[3] One can speak intelligibly about

---

[1]John Maynard Keynes (1936). *The General Theory of Employment, Interest and Money*, London: Macmillan Cambridge University Press, for Royal Economic Society.

[2]Irving Fisher (1930). *The Theory of Interest*, Augustus M Kelley.

[3]Robert Barro (1989). "The Ricardian approach to budget deficits," *The Journal of Economic Perspectives*, Vol. 3, No. 2. http://www.ukzn.ac.za/economics/viegi/teaching/uct/barro.pdf. There is a considerable literature on the microfoundations of macroeconomics. See for

business cycles, growth and monetary "macroeconomic" trends, but they are all deducible from core rational micro-utility optimizing. Growth, for example, is the logical consequence of rational utility-seeking innovation and technological progress. Likewise, business cycles reflect the sum of individual adjustments to unanticipated short term changes in the patterns of demand and supply possibilities just like other types of "natural" short run imperfections.

The "Keynesian revolution" was revolutionary precisely because it broke radically with the rational idealist insistence that optimizing assures nearly perfect results without rejecting sub-optimization. Keynes argued that "income effects" associated with inept attempts at optimally responding to random shocks often caused depressions. They were the enemies within the rational universe, not exogenous forces attributable to human folly like "irrational exuberance."[4] He declared at the beginning of Chapter 1 that:

I have called this book the *General Theory of Employment, Interest and Money*, placing the emphasis on the prefix *general*. The object of such a title is to contrast the character of my arguments and conclusions with those of the classical theory of the subject, upon which I was brought up and which dominates the economic thought, both practical and theoretical, of the governing and academic classes of this generation, as it has for a hundred years past. I shall argue that the postulates of the classical theory are applicable to a special case *only* and not to the general case, the situation which it assumes being a limiting point of the possible positions of equilibrium. Moreover, the characteristics of the special case assumed by the classical theory happen not to be those of the economic society in

example, E. Roy Weintraub (1977). "The Microfoundations of Macroeconomics: A Critical Survey," *Journal of Economic Literature*, Vol. 15, No. 1, pp. 1–23. Weintraub (1979). *Microfoundations: The Compatibility of Microeconomics and Macroeconomics*, Cambridge: Cambridge University Press. Robert Barro (2007). *Macroeconomics: A Modern Approach*, Cambridge: MIT Press and Robert Lucas (1987). *Modern Business Cycles*, Oxford: Basil Blackwell.

[4]Alan Greenspan (December 5, 1996). "The Challenge of Central Banking in a Democratic Society," (speech to the Federal Reserve Bank). Cf. Robert Shiller (2000). *Irrational Exuberance*, Princeton NJ: Princeton University Press. Cf. Alan Greenspan (November/December 2013). "Never Saw it Coming," *Foreign Affairs*, where he claims that he disregarded "animal spirits" in 2008, despite his own warnings about "irrational exuberance." http://www.foreignaffairs.com/articles/140161/alan-greenspan/never-saw-it-coming.

which we actually live, with the result that its teaching is misleading and disastrous if we attempt to apply it to the facts of experience.[5]

Keynes also made allowance for what Herbert Simon was later to call bounded rationality, that is, various satisficing deviations from strict rational idealism like "liquidity traps," which subsequently became staples of macroeconomic theory.

The essence of Keynes's hypothesis is that large, unanticipated drops in aggregate effective demand (the sum of all individual expenditures) perplex profit-seeking suppliers who cannot calibrate the appropriate mix of price, wage and employment adjustments required to restore full voluntary employment equilibrium.[6] They sometimes dismiss too many workers and cut wages excessively, causing effective purchasing power to plummet despite competitive price discounting. These initial dismissals swiftly trigger a negative "multiplier" chain reaction culminating in a depression with mass involuntary unemployment that will persist unless the government deficit spends.

The importance of Keynes's claim doesn't lie in his discovery of a complete explanation for depressions and business cycles. His "multiplier" concept, borrowed from Richard Kahn,[7] has been embellished,[8] and others have suggested additional causes like "irrational pessimism."

The *General Theory* constituted a paradigm shift because it exposed the dysfunctional possibilities of rational optimizing. The Philosophes' optimism was wrong! Unfettered free enterprise doesn't guarantee harmonious endings because of a 19th vulnerable neoclassical axiom. It isn't true that rational competition always provides market participants with the clear signals needed to support generally competitive full employment outcomes.

---

[5] Keynes, *Ibid.*, p. 3.

[6] Steven Rosefielde (2002). *Comparative Economic Systems: Culture, Wealth and Power in the 21st Century*, Blackwell.

[7] Keynes collaborated with Kahn and acknowledged him in his *The General Theory of Employment, Interest and Money*. See Richard Kahn (1931). "The Relation of Home Investment to Unemployment," *Economic Journal*, Vol. 41, No. 162, pp. 173–198. Like Keynes, Kahn was knighted in 1946 for his contributions to economics.

[8] Paul Samuelson (May 1939). "The Interaction Between the Multiplier Analysis and the Principle of Acceleration," *Review of Economic Statistics*, Vol. 21, No. 2, pp. 75–.

This opens up three cans of worms. First, economists need to worry about the completeness of the new macroeconomic optimizing paradigm. Second, they need to integrate not-for-profit government and institutional "satisficing" into what otherwise is a pure optimization construct. Not-for-profit institutions and governments as shown in Chapter 8 typically behave incompatibly with rational utilitarian optimizing because they ride roughshod over consumer sovereignty employing coercive methods to achieve non-Paretian ends. This makes them more apt to exacerbate than cure macroeconomic disequilibria.

Third, once not-for-profit satisficing is incorporated in macrotheory there no longer is any justification for disregarding private sector bounded rationality, or for ignoring other omitted motivations like economic coercion and power-seeking.

Divine Coincidence

Nonetheless, the neoclassical faith in optimality isn't easily dispelled. The enduring impact of rationalist idealism on contemporary macroeconomic theory is manifest in the "divine coincidence" doctrine that dominated professional opinion before the 2008 financial crisis and the recovery polices advocated thereafter. Influenced by Robert Lucas and Phil Kydland and Edward Prescott,[9] the conventional wisdom 2000–2008 came to hold that business cycle oscillations were primarily caused by productivity shocks that lasted until price- and wage-setters disentangled real from nominal effects. These shocks sometimes generated inflation believed to be best addressed with monetary policy. Accordingly, central bankers were tasked with the mission of maintaining slow and stable, Phillips' Curve compatible inflation. Although, central bankers were supposed to be less concerned with real economic activity, many became convinced that full employment and two percent inflation could be sustained indefinitely by

---

[9]Phillip Kydland and Edward Prescott (1982). "Time to Build and Aggregate Fluctuations", *Econometrica*, Vol. 50, No. 6, pp. 1345–1370. Robert Lucas, Jr. (1972). "Expectations and the Neutrality of Money", *Journal of Economic Theory*, Vol. 4, No. 2, pp. 103–124. Robert Lucas Jr. (2003). "Macroeconomic Priorities," *American Economic Review*, Vol. 93, No. 1, pp. 1–14.

"divine coincidence."[10] This miracle was said to be made all the better by the discovery that real economic performance could be regulated with a single monetary instrument, the short term interest rate. Happily, arbitrage across time meant that central bankers could control all temporal interest rates, and arbitrage across asset classes implied that the U.S. Federal Reserve could similarly influence risk adjusted rates for diverse securities. Fiscal policy, which had ruled the roost under the influence of orthodox Keynesianism from 1950–1980 in this way, was relegated to a subsidiary role aided by theorists' faith in the empirical validity of Ricardian equivalence arguments, and skepticism about lags and political priorities.[11] The financial sector likewise was given short shrift, but this still left room for other kinds of non-monetary intervention. The consensus view held that automatic stabilizers like unemployment insurance should be retained to share risks in case there were any unpredictable shocks. Commercial bank credit similarly continued to be regulated, and federal deposit insurance preserved to deter bank runs, but otherwise finance was lightly supervised; especially "shadow banks", hedge funds and derivatives.

This assemblage of attitudes deftly accommodates Keynes's twin faiths in the power of optimizing reason to generate Pareto efficient results in the real economy (non-monetary utilitarian optimization) with his contention that risk-averse firms have a tendency to under employ workers whenever the optimal mix of wage, price and product adjustment is difficult to discern. In the "divine coincidence" variant fiscal policy is deemed ineffectual at low levels of unemployment, but monetary policy designed to generate a two percent rate of inflation perpetually ensures complete optimizing equilibrium in the real economy. A small dose of money illusion is the only theoretical concession needed to reassure concerned Philosophes, without forcing them to confront more troublesome issues posed by bounded rationality, satisficing and other excluded motives.

Six years after the 2008 financial crisis "divine coincidence" is viewed as a quaint conceit. The American and European economies as should have been expected failed to perform according to Lucas's script, swooning into

---

[10]The term refers to situations where stabilizing inflation is the same as stabilizing output.
[11]See Paul De Grauwe (2010), "Top-Down versus Bottom-Up Macroeconomics," *CESifo Economic Studies*, Vol. 56, No. 4 , pp. 465–497.

depressions that have proven stubbornly resistant to double doses of heavy deficit spending and brisk monetary expansion (Bernanke's QE-infinity).[12] The economic damage has been painful, but not intense enough to prompt a fundamental rethinking of rational utilitarian idealism. Theoreticians, particularly those close to the policymaking establishment are content to quarrel about the optimal amount of fiscal and monetary stimulus in optimizing terms, blaming liquidity traps for the slowness of the full recovery still confidently anticipated on good old neoclassical grounds.[13]

---

[12]QE-Infinity refers to Federal Reserve Chairman Ben Bernanke's announcement September 13, 2012 of an open-ended commitment to purchase 40 billion dollars of mortgage-backed securities monthly effectively increasing the Treasury's ability to print money. http://www.investingdaily.com / 15991 / the-fed-expands-qe-infinity-and-directly-targets-inflation-and-employment.

[13]Paul Krugman (2009). *The Return of Depression Economics and the Crisis of 2008*, New York: W.W. Norton Company. Keynes always favored government stimulus. Before 1936 he argued for loose money and credit; afterward he emphasized deficit spending. His disciples have embraced both at the expense of free enterprise. See John Maynard Keynes (1920). *The Economic Consequences of the Peace*, New York: Harcourt Brace.

Chapter 8

Governance

Reason and Government

The Philosophes believed that people are comprehensively rational and contemporary neoclassical idealists uphold the tradition in hard and soft forms. They do so explicitly for the market and treat governance as a natural extension, despite Adam Smith's well known reservations.[1] Rationality as they see it shouldn't stop at the market's edge,[2] an attitude shared by many modern philosophers of science.[3]

---

[1] Adam Smith (1776). *Inquiry into the Nature and Causes of the Wealth of Nations*, London: W. Strahan and T. Cadell.

[2] Enlightenment thinkers like Emmanuel Kant (*Answering the Question: What is Enlightenment?*, 1784) argued for the free unimpeded use of one's own intelligence as a superior guide to righteous behavior, justice and the optimal design of human institutions compatible with the "rights of man" (*French Declaration of the Rights of Man and the Citizen*, 1789). Just at the moment when European monarchs were claiming to rule by "divine right of kings," Enlightenment philosophers insisted democracy was better (John Locke, Jean-Jacques Rousseau, Montesquieu), and when the French Revolution erupted many interpreted the event as the harbinger of impending global democracy. Perry Anderson (1974). *Lineages of the Absolutist State*, London: Verso. Michael Kimmenl (1988). *Absolutism and Its Discontents: State and Society in Seventeenth-Century France and England*, New Brunswick, NJ: Transaction Books. Hillary Zmora (2001). *Monarchy, Aristocracy, and the State in Europe — 1300–1800*, New York: Routledge. Milan Zafirovski (2001). *The Enlightenment and its Effect on Modern Society*.

[3] Alexander Rosenberg (1994). *Mathematic Politics or Science of Diminishing Returns*, Chicago: University of Chicago Press. Alex Rosenberg and Tyler Curtain, "What is Economics Good For?" *The Stone*, August 24, 2013. They claim: "Hobbes and, later, Hume — along with modern philosophers like John Rawls and Robert Nozick — recognized that an economic approach had much to contribute to the design and creative management of such institutions. Fixing bad economic and political institutions (concentrations of power,

Rational beings should apply scientific principles to everything they do without arbitrary boundaries to obtain best results. This obliges them to design and adopt institutions and governance systems that harness competitive markets wherever possible and employ analogous optimal planning, management, regulation, incentives and bureaucratic administration everywhere else to maximize public sector value-added.[4]

The analyses provided in Chapters 4–7 however suggest that managed government markets are unlikely to outperform the private sector. Politicians, program directors, regulators and administrators if anything, are more prone to violate the 19 vulnerable axioms of neoclassical theory than consumers and businessmen subject to the competitive market test. Nonetheless, does the "cunning of reason" somehow assure generally felicitous outcomes?[5]

Bounded Rationality

Many politicians, neoclassical economic theorists, social scientists and humanists express confidence that governments do the right thing. This holds universally for all kinds of government including local, national, supranational, international and global. Some insist that public management often is better than markets on efficiency or normative grounds; others like Joseph Stalin and Kim Jong-un that state planning is comprehensively superior and even ideal.

Few neoclassical economists agree with Stalin and most argue as Adam Smith did that not-for profit institutions are prone to be severely inefficient because the heuristics they employ are primitive and self-serving. Politicians can pick people's pockets (tax) and compel ("mandate") them to obey (rather than satisfice), subject to diverse formal and informal constraints

---

collusions and monopolies), improving good ones (like the Fed's open-market operations), designing new ones (like electromagnetic bandwidth auctions), in the private and public sectors, are all attainable tasks of economic theory." Cf. Karl Popper (1945). *The Open Society and Its Enemies* (2 Volumes), London: Routledge; Popper (1983). *Realism and the Aim of Science*, W.W. Bartley III (ed.), London: Hutchinson.

[4]Robert Dorfman, Paul Samuelson and Robert Solow (1958). *Linear Programming and Economic Analysis*, New York: McGraw Hill.

[5]Georg Wilhelm Friedrich Hegel (2004). *Phenomenology of Spirit*, London: Oxford University Press.

(popular consent). The more coercive and self-serving the not-for-profit regime, the greater the utilitarian loss assessed from the bounded rational market benchmark.

These losses follow rigorously from the heuristic insights of realist neoclassical theory. Governments only talk about optimal decision making; they don't do it.[6] Authorities constrain individual consumer and labor utility choice by mandating the purchase of specific products (ObamaCare),[7] prohibiting various types of consumption (*marijuna*), regulating conditions and terms of employment, and controlling access to public services. Households and workers may be given some choice, but substitution possibilities sometimes are very restrictive. Consumers aren't sovereign. They have "consumer choice," but not "consumer sovereignty" outside the market, and consequently cannot comprehensively optimize utility as the Philosophes hoped.

The efficiency situation on production side (state programs and transfers) is worse. Governments don't operate on a for-profit, or a Baumol-type optimizing basis (see Chapter 5). Their revenue streams depend primarily on taxation, borrowing and printing money, and they are under no pressure to competitively minimize cost.[8] Likewise, public service providers have no knowledge of individuals' desire (preferences) and demand functions, forcing administrators to rely on ambiguous indicators of individual utility and need.

Virtuous institutions and governments recognizing that their satisficing activities are largely detached from rational competitive guidance (including Baumol-type revenue maximizing) may restrain their impulse

---

[6]Domenico Mario Nuti, "Euroarea: Premature, Diminished, Divergent," *Transition*, August 7, 2013. http://dmarionuti.blogspot.it/2013/08/euroarea-premature-diminished-divergent.html.

[7]ObamaCare, alternately called the affordable health care act is an unfolding disaster for young adults who premiums in many cases have catapulted 81%. See Matthew Herper (December 6, 2013). "ObamaCare Raises Health Insurance Premiums, Especially for the Young, *Forbes*. http://www.forbes.com/sites/matthewherper/2013/12/05/obamacare-raises-health-insurance-costs-especially-for-the-young/.

[8]Robert Rector (January 7, 2014). "How the War on Poverty Was Lost: Fifty years and $20 trillion later, LBJ's goal to help the poor become self-supporting has failed," *Wall Street Journal*. http://online.wsj.com/news/article_email/SB10001424052702303345104579282760272285556-lMyQjAxMTA0MDAwODEwNDgyWj.

to oversupply services, but even in the best case temptations to do more than Enlightenment rationality warrants often is irresistible.[9]

The danger has been widely noted with few positive results.[10] Governments and institutions continue to constrict the scope of free individual utility-seeking, pretending that the shortcoming of neoclassical markets oblige them to oversupply public services.[11] Pareto isn't welcome.

Enlightenment thinkers and contemporary rational idealists have always known this; that their faith in the universal perfection of reason rested on shaky footings, but have been reluctant to abandon their conviction. Their solution, when the issue is broached has been to variously claim that not-for-profit institutions and governments are or can be perfected ("doing the right thing"),[12] or made as good as humanly possible (given the state of nature). Kantian assurances of this sort make it seem that not-for-profit institutions and governments are almost as efficient as markets; however, one important element is missing. There is no profit maximizing and utility optimizing invisible hand.

---

[9]Anticompetitiveness degrades both micro and macroeconomic efficiency. Nassim Nicholas Taleb has compiled a list of the macro risks for western economies: (1) "too-big-to-fail" notions; (2) the socialization of losses and privatization of gains; (3) "nothing succeeds like failure" attitudes; (4) incentivizing regulatory incompetents to manage risk; (5) excessive complexity; (6) empowering government to play with matches; (7) allowing government to play the confidence-building con game; (8) giving government excess-spending addicts further doses to assuage their pain; (9) canonizing charlatan experts; (10) patchwork reform used as a substitute for fundamental systems redesign. Nassim Taleb (2007). *Black Swan: The Impact of the Highly Improbable*. New York: Random House.

[10]James Buchanan and Robert Tollison (1975). *The Limits of Liberty Between Anarchy and Leviathan*, Chicago: University of Chicago Press. S. Ross (1973). "The Economic Theory of Agency: The Principal's Problem," *American Economic Review*, Vol. 63, pp. 134–139. Eric Maskin, and Jean Tirole (1990). "The Principal–Agent Relationship with an Informed Principal, I: Private Values," *Econometrica*, Vol. 58, pp. 379–410. Eric Maskin, and Jean Tirole (1992). "The Principal–Agent Relationship with an Informed Principal, II: Common Values," *Econometrica*, Vol. 60, pp. 1–42. Tracy Lewis and David Sappington (1993). "Ignorance in Agency Problems," *Journal of Economic Theory*, Vol. 61, pp. 169–183. Jean-Jacques Laffont, and Jean Tirole (1993). *A Theory of Incentives in Procurement and Regulation*, MIT Press, Cambridge.

[11]Steven Rosefielde and Quinn Mills (2013). *Democracy and its Elected Enemies*, Cambridge University Press: Cambridge.

[12]Georg Wilhelm Friedrich Hegel, *Phenomenology of Spirit,* tr. A. V. Miller, 1977 on contending theories of humans as fully self-sufficient individuals and social beings.

Adam Smith, recognizing that rational utilitarian self-seekers might harm others, undercutting confidence in the universal beneficence of reason, reassured himself and fellow economists that competition would save the day. Does an analogous optimizing solution exist for the non-profit public sector? The answer is no. Institutions and governmental public service providers cannot obtain direct knowledge of optimal competitive outcomes by simulating markets to stop people from willy-nilly raiding the public larder and evading their tax obligations.[13] Soviet planners in the late 1980s sought to do this, but informational and computational barriers soon proved insuperable to any satisfactory degree of approximation.[14]

Nothing in optimizing or satisficing versions of neoclassical theory justifies the presumption that neoclassical theory guided government assures that we live in "the best of all possible worlds,"[15] or that outcomes are acceptable.[16] Leibniz was wrong in the 18th century,[17] and his disciples are wrong today.

---

[13]Linear programming claims to sidestep profit maximizing by substituting utilities or prices in primal objective functions, but these values are unknown and unknowable. Other objectives like revenue maximizing are only indirectly connected with utility.

[14]Steven Rosefielde (2007). *Russian Economy from Lenin to Putin*, New York: Wiley. Egon Neuberger (March 1966). "Libermanism, Computopia and the Visible Hand: The Question of Informational Efficiency," *American Economic Review*, Vol. 56, No. ½.

[15]The phrase "the best of all possible worlds" was coined by Gottfried Leibniz *in Essais de Theodicee sur la bonte de Dieu, la liberte de l'homme et l'origine du mal*, 1710. Since God is good and omnipotent, and since He chose this world out of all possibilities, this world must be good — in fact, this world is the best of all possible worlds.

[16]This inference applies by extension to various idealist neoclassical schemes like worker managed economies that rely on neoclassical axioms. See Evsey Domar (September 1966). "The Soviet Collective Farm as a Producer Cooperative," *American Economic Review*, Vol. 56, No. 4, pp. 734–757. Benjamin, Ward (September 1958). "The Firm in Illyria: Market Syndicalism," *American Economic Review*, Vol. 48, No. 4, pp. 566–589. Martin Weitzman (1986). *The Share Economy*, Harvard University Press, Cambridge Steven Rosefielde and R. W. Pfouts (June 1986). "The Firm in Illyria: Market Syndicalism Revisited," *Journal of Comparative Economics*, Vol. 10, No. 2, pp. 160–170.

[17]Russell, Bertrand (1900). *A Critical Exposition of the Philosophy of Leibniz*, London: George Allen & Unwin.

Chapter 9

Democracy

Democratic Governance

No sovereign government is completely efficient because all violate ideal neoclassical theory's basic 19 axioms. Democracy isn't immune.[1]

---

[1] Democracy literally means people's rule (*demos kratos*); a governance system where the political sovereignty of everyman reigns without privilege or special entitlement. The Greek word *demos* and the English equivalent people are collective singulars (pluralities of human beings) which retain the double sense of heterogeneous individual persons and their oneness. The duality is easily grasped, but also can be a source of ambiguity because the sense determines the meaning of *kratos*. If the term is used as a synonym for nation without regard for individuality, then democracy is a shallow concept meaning little more than any kind of governance in the national "interest." Alternatively, if the *demos* is a collection of heterogeneous persons (of the people), who elect representatives and participate in governing (by the people), with the purpose of bettering themselves individually and collectively (for the people), then the term acquires all the modern meanings of freely competitive multiparty, elected, civic participatory state governance serving the heterogeneous needs of minority rights protected citizens. Democracy, particular in the American setting is a type of republic, where the people don't carry out the tasks of government directly by themselves, but delegate this job to elected representatives, controlled by the people through periodic elections and the constitution. See James Madison, *Federalist Paper* No. 10. The American republic is a representative democracy. The term *republic* does not appear in the Declaration of Independence, but does appear in Article IV of the Constitution which "guarantee[s] to every State in this Union a Republican form of Government." What exactly the writers of the constitution felt this should mean is uncertain. The Supreme Court, in *Luther v. Borden* (1849), declared that the definition of *republic* was a "political question" in which it would not intervene. In two later cases, it did establish a basic definition. In *United States v. Cruikshank* (1875), the court ruled that the "equal rights of citizens" were inherent to the idea of republic.

All sovereign governments satisfice, but only one type tries to minimize the losses attributable to command, planning, management, regulation and administration by relying wherever possible on the market. The optimal size of democratic governance is elastic, and depends on the people's demand for public services and transfers. Uncharitable or charitable majorities may task representative governments to efficiently provide smaller or larger volumes of public services, subject to minority civil and private property right protections. We call this elastic system "true democracy" because it extends the principle of consumer sovereignty in the private sector to the provision of public goods, services and transfers.[2] The archetype is America's 1787 constitution.

Kenneth Arrow provided the foundation for the presumption that markets are superior to democratic government as goods and services providers by demonstrating that the informational content of balloting is lower than free market negotiation.[3] The bounded rationality of government (including democratic social choice and coalitions) is greater than free

---

However, the term republic is not synonymous with the republican form. The republican form is defined as one in which the powers of sovereignty are vested in the people and are exercised by the people, either directly, or through representatives chosen by the people, to whom those powers are specially delegated.

[2] Steven Rosefielde and Quinn Mills (2013). *Democracy and its Elected Enemies*, Cambridge: Cambridge University Press.

[3] Kenneth Arrow (August 1950)." A Difficulty in the Concept of Social Welfare," *Journal of Political Economy*, Vol. 58, No. 4, pp. 328–246. Arrow (1951). *Social Choice and Individual Values*, New York: Wiley; Arrow's demonstration that balloting doesn't provide faithful democratic representatives with sufficient information to always act in accordance with the majority's will is commonly referred to as Arrow's "impossibility theorem," or "Arrow's paradox." Kotaro Suzumura, Kenneth Arrow, Amartya Sen (eds.) (2002), *Handbook of Social Choice and Welfare*, Vol. 1, Amsterdam: Elsevier. The theorem states that when voters have three or more distinct alternatives, no rank order voting system can convert the ranked preferences of individuals into a community-wide (complete and transitive) ranking while also meeting the criteria of unrestricted domain, non-dictatorship, Pareto efficiency, and interdependence of irrelevant alternatives. There are problems with Arrow's numerical demonstration. See Eric Maskin's introduction in Kenneth Arrow, *Social Choice and Individual Values*, Princeton: Princeton University Press, 2012. The authors don't accept the adequacy of Arrow's proof.

enterprise, a finding compatible with Simon's realist conception of neo-classical theory.[4]

This presumption of superior market efficiency moreover is strengthened by the further problem of faithful agency. The existence of true democracy and the merit of alternative balloting regimes generally depend on faithful agency, which constitutes another fundamental neoclassical axiom, the 20th.

Faithful Agency

The people cannot be their own government because it is impractical to perpetually vote on every public decision. Guild socialists like G. D. H. Cole in the early 20th century briefly imagined that industrial democracy was viable,[5] but their dreams came to naught. Democratic national government inevitably is representative. Voters elect representatives to act as their agents, with minimal discretionary authority. Insofar as possible, representatives are supposed to faithfully implement the people's instructions. Otherwise, they are required to act in good faith as they believe the people desire. Representatives should never promote their own self-interest over the people's will because this violates the principle of consumer (electorate) sovereignty, transferring sovereignty from the people to their agents, *de facto*. Representatives often claim that balloting permits them to "lead" because they govern by popular "consent,"[6] not popular will, but government ceases being democratic the moment authority is usurped by representatives on this, or any other pretext. Democracy as

---

[4]Amartya Sen counter-argues that the loss here may not be great because Pareto optimality itself is a contestable ideal, a point already made by Abram Bergson in the 1930s. See Amartya Sen (1979), "Personal Utilities and Public Judgements: Or What's Wrong with Welfare Economics," *Economic Journal*, Vol. 89, No. 355, pp. 537–588.

[5]George Douglas Howard Cole (1919), *Self-Government in Industry*, London: G. Bell, 1917. Cole (1920), *Guild Socialism Re-Stated*, London: L. Parsons.

[6]Buchanan and Tullock suggest that the problem can be mitigated by requiring that government programs only be undertaken when approved by unanimous workable public consent. James Buchana and Robert Tollison (1975). *The Limits of Liberty Between Anarchy and Leviathan*, Chicago: University of Chicago Press. James Buchanan (1999). *Democracy in Deficit: The Political Legacy of Lord Keynes*, Indianapolis, IN: Liberty Fund.

the Philosophes conceived it requires faithful agency;[7] that the *demos* be *kratos*.

Both idealist and realist neoclassical theory are vulnerable on this score. Representatives construed broadly to include the legislative, executive and judicial branches of government often are derelict in the execution of their duties. They impose their own for the people's assessment of "the greater good", or act in their own self-interest. The first motive is paternalist; the second is selfish, immoral, or criminal depending on the circumstances. Motives vary, but in all instances representatives succumb to "moral hazard"; they fall prey to temptation invalidating idealist neoclassical theory of democratic governance, and in many cases the realist neoclassical outlook too. The greater the scale of the abuse, the worse the outcome.[8]

This is hardly a secret,[9] but has had little impact on Enlightenment intellectuals' faith in the power of reason to yield superior results regardless of occasional legislative, presidential and judicial lapses.[10] Reason may

---

[7] S. Ross (1973). "The Economic Theory of Agency: The Principal's Problem," *American Economic Review*, Vol. 63, pp. 134–139. E. Maskin and J. Tirole (1990). "The Principal–Agent Relationship with an Informed Principal, I: Private Values," *Econometrica*, Vol. 58, pp. 379–410. E. Makin and J. Tirole (1992). "The Principal–Agent Relationship with an Informed Principal, II: Common Values," *Econometrica*, Vol. 60, pp. 1–42. T. and D. Sappington (1993). "Ignorance in Agency Problems," *Journal of Economic Theory*, Vol. 61, pp. 169–183. J. J. Laffont, and J. Tirole (1993). *A Theory of Incentives in Procurement and Regulation*, Cambridge MA: MIT Press. Steven Rosefielde (2012). "The Impossibility of Russian Economic Reform: Waiting for Godot," in Stephen Blank (ed.), *Russian Reform*, Carlisle Barracks: US Army War College.

[8] Steven Rosefielde and Quinn Mills (2013). *Democracy and Its Elected Enemies*, Cambridge: Cambridge University Press.

[9] All of these disorders were grasped in their essentials by Enlightenment democrats like John Locke and America's founding fathers, and the safeguards they recommended remain valid.

[10] Judicial defense of constitutional principle can be degraded in two ways. Courts can bend the meaning of constitutional provisions for diverse purposes, and legislatures can overwhelm the system with contradictory laws that give judges license for corruption. The first abuse is connected with the concept of the "living constitution." It asserts that constitutional meanings are dynamic and should be interpreted according to contemporary norms, allowing courts to override constitutional protections. The principle is often applied to the equal protection and due process clauses of the 5th and 14th Amendments to the American constitution. David Weigel, "Ruth Bader Ginsburg Makes Banal Point, Destroys the Republic," "I would not look to the US constitution, if I were drafting a constitution in the year 2012."

prevail, and when it does neoclassical theory is right enough. However, if inefficiencies are large and democratic sovereignty is usurped, Simon's bounded rationality becomes an inadequate guide on both positive and normative grounds,[11] and needs to be augmented with supplementary neo-realist constructs.

---

[11]Abram Bergson (1938). "A Reformulation of Certain Aspects of Welfare Economics," *Quarterly Journal of Economics*, Vol. 52, No. 1, pp. 310–334. Bergson (1954). "The Concept of Social Welfare," *Quarterly Journal of Economics*, Vol. 68, No. 2, pp. 233–253. Bergson (1976). "Social Choice Under Representative Government", *Journal of Public Economics*, Vol. 6, No. 3, pp. 171–190.

Part II

Neo-realist Economics

Chapter 10

When Reason Fails

The broad neoclassical consensus that competitive markets and governments yield good results rests on the premise that realist heuristics are sound and human motives are mostly rational and benevolent. Reason prevails. The outlook reflects a continuing faith in the power of Enlightenment reason in the face of counterclaims that men are sometimes foolish, demented and immoral.

However, suppose that reason fails; that faith in Enlightenment reason is overdrawn because men occasionally are imprudent, impulsive, corrupt, or simply don't what to live according Pareto-efficient competitive principles. What happens then?

This is the domain of neo-realist economic theory, where bounded rationality and sound heuristics aren't enough to assure that satisficing yields acceptable results. It covers all cases where reason is insufficient to guarantee desirable neoclassical outcomes, even in the presence of workably competitive price attractors and heuristic surrogates for optimal decision making. Welcome to the world of neo-realism, where reason by itself isn't strong enough to provide sky blue lives for anyone; only gray existences for some, and bleak ones for others. People outside the precincts of neoclassical Eden aren't assiduous, fully rational, competitive utility maximizers in the labor, production, finance, and distribution markets, abiding by Lockean social contracts. They don't optimally innovate, invest and consume. They don't maximize wellbeing at every moment, and cumulatively over their lifetimes.

When reason fails, people are unreasonable. Driven by undisciplined desires and prodded by the powerful, many are under-productive, exploited, unfulfilled and discontent. Individuals are conflicted, households quarrelsome, communities disharmonious, societies antagonistic, nations contentious and international relations combustible. There are exceptions, moments of amity, affection, caring and rapture, but also immense anxiety, poverty, discord and injustice that cannot be cured by rational neoclassical methods until sanity is restored.

Neoclassical methods are of little avail if men are unreasonable precisely because they are predicated on 20 false rational axioms. When reason fails and these 20 axioms are violated, neoclassical theory becomes impotent.

The problem runs very deep. Economists relying on Enlightenment nostrums take it for granted not only that people have well defined, transitively ordered preferences (axiom 1), but that these preferences and orderings are rationally formed (axiom 7). When reason fails, neither supposition is true. People cannot successfully apply reason to evaluate the merit of their preferences, and their malformed priorities cannot be coherently ordered. This prevents unreasonable individuals and officials from coping effectively with the challenges confronting them. People needlessly suffer, and cannot be protected from themselves because families, communities, societies and governments are similarly benighted. It may be comforting to suppose that benevolent authorities will always come to the rescue, but in unreasonable times it is illogical to expect custodians to be saner than the inmates.

The problem also is profound because when reason fails normative economics is incapacitated (see Appendix 1).[1] This is a corollary of the

---

[1]Abram Bergson (1938). "A Reformulation of Certain Aspects of Welfare Economics," *Quarterly Journal of Economics*, Vol. 52, No. 1, pp. 310–334. Bergson (1954). "The Concept of Social Welfare," *Quarterly Journal of Economics*, Vol. 68, No. 2, pp. 233–253. Abram Bergson (1976). "Social Choice Under Representative Government," *Journal of Public Economics*, Vol. 6, No. 3, pp. 171–190. Neoclassical theory only addresses the issue of micro-merit in its normative (welfare) branch, where Pareto efficient outcomes are treated as one important standard of virtue among numerous rivals. Abram Bergson in collaboration with Paul Samuelson first formulated this normative concept in 1938. The merit of any individual outcome or system can be calibrated with normative functions (which they called

falsification of axiom 7. Although, it has been common knowledge since Socrates that no uniquely superior system of ethics can be constructed because numerous plausible premises cannot be reconciled (paradox),[2] the concept of wisdom has always been applied to distinguish superior from inferior ways of proceeding.[3] Sages divine the right course of action by combining intellect with perceptions, emotions, values and knowledge.[4] When reason fails, people may act on their perceptions, emotions, values and knowledge, but this will never be enough to provide wise results. Individuals and leaders per force must be adrift. People with failed reason cannot accurately judge how to conduct themselves, or intelligently apply normative methods to assess social welfare, and consequently sometimes rationalize reprehensible behavior including Stalin's and Pol Pot's crimes against humanity.[5]

---

social welfare functions), given the appraiser's scale of value. Algebraically,

$$W = F(U_1, U_2, U_3, Un; \ x, y, z)$$

where

U_i = the cumulative utility experienced by the ith individual over some interval
x, y, z = any relational determinants of utility such as civil liberties and equality, or other judgmental factors that affect the observer's detailed assessment of merit.
F = a value forming function aggregating individual utilities generated directly from consumption and indirectly from the relational-judgmental variables.

The Bergsonian W can be a point estimate, or interpreted as a set of "welfare" curves (iso-merit), analogous to consumer iso-utility curves as previously discussed in Appendix 1. However, construed, they always assume that judges are wise, that they comprehensively and scrupulously employ critical reason to soundly evaluate merit according to the "right" ethics as they perceive them. Men and women of good faith frequently will place different values on the same set of outcomes, but this cannot be remedied because there is no universally accepted canon of Kantian categorical imperatives. The best that can be done is to engage in democratic discussions to try and find common ground.

[2]Reginald E. Allen (2006). *Plato: The Republic*. New Haven: Yale University Press.
[3]Athena was the goddess of wisdom and the chief goddess of Athens. Robert Sternberg (1990). *Wisdom: Its Nature, Origins, and Development*, Cambridge: Cambridge University Press.
[4]Cf. Jurgen Habermas (1990). *Moral Consciousness and Communicative Action*, MIT Press: Cambridge, MA. Habermas (1984). *Theory of Communicative Action Volume One: Reason and the Rationalization of Society*, Beacon Press: Boston.
[5]Steven Rosefielde (2010). *Red Holocaust*, New York: Routledge.

Unreasonableness unfortunately is more the norm than the exception because people have immense powers of self-deception. Individuals and leaders ceaselessly rationalize their motives and actions to themselves and others, and so tilt at windmills instead of optimizing individual utility and social welfare. Consequently, potentials that could easily be attained remain forever out of reach because people indulge themselves in wishful thinking.[6] Ironically, neoclassical theorists often contribute to neoclassical theory's failing because they prefer to pretend that people are rational rather than pressing them to become reasonable.

Neo-realist theory doesn't require that everyone be unreasonable, or uniformly diminished, and there may be moments of lucidity. All that is needed to switch from the neoclassical to the neo-realist universe is for the unreasonableness of some to dominate the behavior of the many. This further clarifies the paradox between what neoclassical theory teaches people ought to do, and how they actually behave. The bad quite simply often repress the good, a situation stressed by political scientists, anthropologists and sociologists that requires sons and daughters of the Enlightenment to try harder.

---

[6]James Traub, review of Nina Munk, *"The Idealist," Wall Street Journal*, September 7, 2013. Munk investigated Jeffrey Sachs's Millennium Fund African project. She discovered that it failed egregiously, and that when confronted by the facts Sachs remained in denial.

Chapter 11

Why Reason Seldom Prevails

The Philosophes (public intellectuals during the Age of Reason) were apostles of reason because they believed in its power to enlighten and deliver mankind from sin and promote freedom and prosperity. They didn't ponder how people determined the utility of their activities and consumption choices (conscious and subconscious thinking), erroneously assuming in pre-modern fashion that every individual could easily devise his or her virtuous preferences. Herbert Simon employing a less stringent notion of utility limited to consistent selection given established preferences also was impressed with the potency of reason, but cautioned that it wasn't a panacea because cognitive and environmental constraints often compelled people to satisfice.[1] He appreciated that this was a narrow reading of

---

[1] Gerd Gigerenzer and Reinhard Selten (2002). *Bounded Rationality: The Adaptive Tool Box*, Cambridge MA: MIT Press. Bounded rationality is the idea that in decision making, rationality of individuals is limited by the information they have, the cognitive limitations of their minds, and the finite amount of time they have to make decisions. It was proposed by Herbert Simon as an alternative basis for the mathematical modeling of decision making, as used in economics and related disciplines; it complements rationality and optimization, which view decision making as a fully rational process of finding an optimal choice given the information available. Another way to look at bounded rationality is that, because decision-makers lack the ability and resources to arrive at the optimal solution, they instead apply their rationality only after having greatly simplified the choices available. Thus the decision-maker is a satisficer, one seeking a satisfactory solution rather than the optimal one. Simon used the analogy of a pair of scissors, where one blade is the "cognitive limitations" of actual humans and the other the "structures of the environment"; minds with limited cognitive resources can thus be successful by exploiting pre-existing structure and regularity in the environment.

"bounded adaptation," that excluded various aspects of human behavior, but didn't probe further.[2] Economics for him as well as most contemporary optimization theorists is primarily about consistent utilitarian selection, regardless of how utility is interpreted or individuals formulate their preferences.[3]

Unfortunately, this handling of utility and inattentiveness to complexities of individual preference formation throw the baby out with the bath water. Both the Philosophes' concept of rationality (including Hegelian divine order),[4] and modern "logically consistent selection" generate false utility possibilities because they mischaracterize utility management by embracing a paradox-free definition of reason, disregard "rationalization," ignore conflicts between reason and desire, and overlook other aspects of human wellbeing. This misleadingly makes it seem as if

1) What feels good is "good for you;[5] that hedonism is wise.[6]
2) Computing marginal utilities is the only justifiable way to consume, even though individuals sometimes derive utility by acting spontaneously rather than by weighing net benefits or haphazardly constructing worthy existences.
3) People diligently utility search, even though they are often impulsive.
4) Preferences are ideal, even though they are frequently warped. If people miss determine their preferences, perfect rational selection cannot save

---

[2]Assumptions don't have to be true. Economists therefore can suppose if they wish that people are reasonable in all senses desired.

[3]Herbert Simon (1955). "A Behavior Model of Rational Choice," *Quarterly Journal of Economics*, Vol. 59, pp. 99–118. Simon (1957). *Models of Man*, New York: Wiley. Simon (1959). "Theories of Decision Making in Economic Behavioral Science," *American Economic Review*, Vol. 49, pp. 99–118. Simon (1982). Models of Bounded Rationality, Cambridge, MA: Harvard University Press. Herbert Simon with M. Egidi, R. Marris and R. Viale, *Economics, Bounded Rationality and the Cognitive Revolution*, Aldershot: Ashgate, 1992.

[4]Georg Wilhelm Friedrich Hegel, *Phenomenology of Spirit*, London: Oxford University Press, 2004. Hegel believed that reason was the dialectical will of God and what was ought to be. Marx borrowed the idea for his theory of class struggle. Both premises are no longer considered credible.

[5]Immanuel Kant (2011). *The Critique of Pure Reason*, New York: CreateSpace Independent Publishing Platform.

[6]Wisdom is discerning the right choice among seemingly equivalent utilitarian alternatives taking added account of complex normative factors including morality.

them from their folly. They will economize the wrong things and fail to truly utility maximize.

These lapses mean that individual and national utilities must be lower than rational choice utilitarian idealists contend because people don't always weigh their options, search diligently, form best preferences, behave ethically and choose wisely.[7] The real world isn't efficient, beneficent, virtuous, harmonious and stable. It is often conflict-ridden, disoriented, wasteful, and corrupt in part because people cannot figure out how best to discover themselves and cooperate harmoniously with others.

False Premises

Martin Heidegger's concept of "being in the world" and Sigmund Freud's psychoanalytic theory provide useful post-Enlightenment frameworks for probing real preference construction. Heidegger takes the position that individuals cannot know themselves and external reality solely through introspection; that they cannot easily ascertain or create realistic rationally ordered preferences and so are compelled to haphazardly discover themselves and their preferences by "involvement" in the world with a discerning eye.[8] They must muster their emotions, intuitions, imaginative, normative and rational faculties, consciously and subconsciously to fathom others and test their concepts of internal and external reality, learning as best they can through trial and error how to construct more gratifying existences.

---

[7]If governments composed of Freud's flawed individuals were miraculously competent, it would be possible for the nation's utility to be higher than might be deduced from the simple sum of individual utilities, but this is implausible.

[8]Martin Heidegger, *Sein und Zeit*, in Heidegger's Gesamtausgabe, volume 2, ed. F.-W. von Herrmann, 1977, XIV. Hubert Dreyfus (1990). *Being-in-the-World: A Commentary on Heidegger's Being and Time, Division I* (Cambridge, Massachusetts, & London: MIT Press. Jean-Paul Sartre (2001). *Being and Nothingness: An Essay in Phenomenological Ontology*, Citadel Press. Hans-Georg Gadamer (2004). *Truth and Method*, 2nd rev. edn. Trans. J. Weinsheimer and D. G. Marshall, New York: Crossroad. "Authenticity" in Heideggar's usage means devoting oneself completely to the pursuit of important goals, instead of going through the motions. This quiets anxiety. Phenomenological and existential philosophy urge people to "be-in-the-world" and thereby links being and anxiety with civilization. In Sartre's case, socialism is worthy civilization, capitalism reprehensible.

This hit and miss process tries to make sense of existential paradox,[9] rationalize illusory conflicting desires and duties, and create worthy identities, but its efficacy is necessarily restricted. "Being in the world" is open-ended (incompatible with deterministic optimization), and partly overlaps with Freud's psychiatric theory of desire and preference.

Freud believed that human intellect was too feeble for people to adequately cope with life's physical and psychological adversities,[10] let alone exhaustively optimize. In his terminology, the "ego" (connected to protean "identity") is supposed to grasp and harmoniously resolve conflicts between a person's "libido" (instincts),[11] and "superego" (conscience),[12] but does a poor job. People cannot satisfactorily manage their primal desires and impractical impulses for instant gratification (the emotions of cognitive psychology), and their equally impractical moral ideals with their limited powers of reason, invention, adaptation and attitude adjustment;[13] a problem compounded by external pressures, warped identities, personality disorders, schizophrenia, neuroses and psychoses.[14] They do not, and cannot

[9]Willard Van Orman Quine (1976). *The Ways of Paradox*, Cambridge MA: Harvard University Press; Quine (1986). *The Philosophy of Logic*, Cambridge MA: Harvard University Press; Quine (1986). *Pursuit of Truth*, Cambridge MA: Harvard University Press.

[10]Intellect is a term used in studies of the human mind, referring to the ability of the mind to reach conclusions about what is true or real, and how to solve technical and psychological problems. Intelligence has a similar meaning, but with a stress placed on understanding more than problem solving.

[11]Instinct is defined as innate non-cognitive and non-conscious behavior that emerges without training or education that provides a partial explanation of human behavior. It may take evolved form in cooperation, sexuality, child rearing, aesthetics and language. David Buss (2008). *Evolutionary Psychology: The New Science of the Mind*, Boston: Omegatype.

The libido is associated with the childlike portion of the brain that operates on the "pleasure principle." Hence, Bentham's utilitarianism in Freud's perspective is infantile behavior.

[12]Sigmund Shlomo Freud, *Beyond the Pleasure Principle*, 1923 and Freud, *The Ego and the Id*, (*Das Ich und das Es*), 1923. This is a late formulation that replaced his prior categories of conscious, unconscious and preconscious.

[13]Freud likened the relationship between the id and the ego to horses (drive) and a charioteer (control), which is suggestive but should be reformulated as horses guided by a neurotic charioteer. D Hothersall, *History of Psychology*, New York: McGraw-Hill, p. 290. Attitude adjustment allows people to cope with disappointed expectations. Instead of changing their behavior they revise the preferences. Leon Festinger (1957). *A Theory of Cognitive Dissonance*, Stanford, CA: Stanford University Press.

[14]Sigmund Shlomo Freud (1930). *Civilization and its Discontents*, [*Das Unbehagen in der Kultur* ("The Uneasiness in Culture")].

fully know their own minds and potentials. They are compelled to adopt illusory short and long term goals (guidelines) and coping strategies shaped indiscriminately by their inadequacies, fantasies, emotions (psychophysiological responses to situational experiences),[15] desires, intuitions,[16] intellect and neuroses that preclude the construction of realistic preferences.

People conceal their contradictory behavior and neuroses from themselves by constructing legitimating personas and identities,[17] and by employing defense mechanisms including denial, repression, displacement and sublimation. They may imagine when "talking to themselves" that they are optimizing across all Freudian mind management possibilities, but they are deluded (rationalization). They may imagine that they are satisficing;[18] but this too is self-deceptive because bounded searching doesn't eliminate the possibility that interim goals and strategies (including drifting) are inferior.[19] There is only a thin line separating the diligent utility searching postulated by rational utilitarian idealists and neurotically chasing rainbows.[20] It can be said that people in free markets do as they please, but this doesn't mean that they optimize, properly satisfice in Herbert Simon's sense, or choose wisely.[21]

---

[15] Derek Denton (2006). *The Primordial Emotions: The Dawning of Consciousness*, London: Oxford University Press. Elaine Fox (2008). *Emotion Science: An Integration of Cognitive and Neuroscientific Approaches*, New York: Palgrave MacMillan.

[16] Jonathan Haidt (2006). *The Happiness Hypothesis: Find Modern Truth in Ancient Wisdom*, New York: Basic Books. Haidt argues that most judgments are quick intuitive evaluations of scenarios.

[17] Peter Burke and Jan E. Stets (2009). *Identity theory*. New York: Oxford Univ. Press.

[18] Bounded rationality is the idea that in decision making, rationality of individuals is limited by the information they have, the cognitive limitations of their minds, and the finite amount of time they have to make decisions.

[19] People who fail to completely utility search are classified as satisficers, if they accept inferior outcomes because they cannot overcome neuroses, and culturally imposed obligations, and recognize at some level that they cannot ascertain how to proceed in anything except the broadest manner. This definition is stronger that Herbert Simon's which amounts to optimizing under probabilistic constraints with incomplete information and weak mental computing powers.

[20] Buddhists similarly scoff at efficiently indulging chimerical desires.

[21] Freud's theory of the mind has been revised by various critiques from humanistic, existential and sociological standpoints. All are interesting, but peripheral to our primary distinction between reason as consistent selection and more emotionally driven choice mechanisms. In the 1950s and 1960s, largely influenced by the work of German philosopher Martin Heidegger and Danish philosopher Søren Kierkegaard, psychoanalytically trained American

Coping

Heidegger's and Freud's caveats about the limits of human rationality falsify neoclassical (as well as Marxist and Austrian aspects) optimizing and satisficing claims of rational utilitarian idealism, but don't exclude the concept of self-betterment seeking. Individuals still try to improve their mental states (Freud's pleasure principle) and logically select in a loose utilitarian manner, but without the rational consistency of neoclassical optimizing and satisficing because they are distracted by life's paradoxes, conundrums, perplexities, desires, pretensions, illusions and unruliness, and/or they dramatize, romanticize, spiritualize, rationalize, fantasize and indulge in other forms of mental escapism (dreams over matter).[22] They "cope with" their psychic conflicts instead of optimizing or satisficing due to limited information and computational abilities.[23]

Those who do the job well may behave more or less as "second best" neoclassical optimizers or satisficers. Some may even be able to discover superior routes to wellbeing. Those who don't, including leaders, write their own peculiar laws of economic action.

---

psychologist Rollo May pioneered an existential branch of psychology, which included existential psychotherapy, a method of therapy that operates on the belief that inner conflict within a person is due to that individual's confrontation with the givens of existence. Existential psychologists differed from others often classified as humanistic in their comparatively neutral view of human nature and in their relatively positive assessment of anxiety. Existential psychologists emphasized the humanistic themes of death, free will, and meaning, suggesting that meaning can be shaped by myths, or narrative patterns and that it can be encouraged by an acceptance of the free will requisite to an authentic, albeit often anxious, regard for death and other future prospects. Austrian existential psychiatrist and Holocaust survivor Viktor Frankel drew evidence of meanin's therapeutic power from reflections garnered from his own internment, and he created a variety of existential psychotherapy called logotherapy, a type of existentialist analysis that focuses on a will to meaning (in one's life), as opposed to Adler's Nietzschean doctrine of will to power or Freud's will to pleasure. Cf. Eric Fromm (1992). *The Revision of Psychoanalysis*, Colorado: Westview Press.

[22]The marginal utility of any good or service from the individual perspective is susceptible to attitude management. This transforms what is supposed to be objective utility maximizing into an indeterminate subjective exercise.

[23] "Coping" unlike satisficing implies reason is incompletely applied to forming preferences and rendering them consistent.

Chapter 12

Dangers

Neo-realism is the theory of diverse forms of aberrant economic behavior judged from the rationalist Enlightenment standard. It encompasses disturbed, corrupt, and sublime behavior as well as acquiescent conflict resolution strategies. All neo-realist behavior is incompatible with idealist Pareto optimality, and most disturbed and corrupt activities are psychological and ethically detrimental, but sublime behavior and acquiescent conflict resolution strategies may have compensating virtues. Wise individuals and societies therefore should cherry pick. They can achieve superior results by eradicating the bad, and harnessing the good.[1] This chapter examines the dangers posed by disturbed and unscrupulous neo-realist behaviors. Chapter 13 analyses opportunities afforded by sublime behavior and acquiescent conflict resolution strategies.

Thwarted Individuals

Benighted individuals ostensibly behave like autonomous utility-seekers. They work, shop, consume and invest and to the untrained eye may appear to satisfy most of neoclassical theory's fundamental axioms, but they march

---

[1]Jonathan Haidt (2013). *The Righteous Mind: Why Good People Are Divided by Politics and Religion*, New York: Vintage.

to a different drummer. The axioms that guide them are:

1) Disturbed individual **preferences are incomplete and haphazardly formulated** (incompletely defined continuous and discrete preferences over a patchwork domain),
2) disturbed individual **preferences are often interpersonally dependent (including irrelevant alternatives)**,
3) disturbed and unscrupulous **individuals miss-select,**
4) disturbed and unscrupulous **individuals miss-search,**
5) disturbed **individuals are often co-dependent** (individuals, households, collectives),
6) disturbed and malign **individuals disregard Adam Smith's pro-competitive moral admonitions**[2] (and Locke's social contract),[3]
7) disturbed and unscrupulous individual **preferences are miss-formed,**
8) **individual wellbeing is diminished by disturbed and unscrupulous marginal choices,**
9) **production and cost functions are not always continuous, twice differentiable and monotonic,**
10) **disturbed suppliers have distorted understanding of demand and intermediate input acquisition possibilities,**
11) **disturbed suppliers have distorted preferences that prevent them from optimizing with discrete production and cost functions, and operate with distorted information on intermediate input supplies and demand,**
12) **disturbed supplier (manager) preferences often are interpersonally dependent,**
13) **disturbed and unscrupulous managers miss-select,**
14) **disturbed managers miss-explore profit and cost minimization possibilities,**
15) disturbed **managers co-dependently choose** (CEOs and collective corporate decision makers),

---

[2]Adam Smith (1759). *Theory of Moral Sentiments*, London.
[3]This is a weak definition of ethics that leaves ample room for normative debate.

16) **disturbed and unscrupulous managers misbehave** within the frame-work of an anti-Lockean social contract,
17) **disturbed and unscrupulous managers' preferences are miss-formed,**
18) **founding institutions are distorted and unscrupulously designed (including property rights),**
19) **disturbed and unscrupulously competitive markets provide mis-information and disinformation that preclude the attainment of generally competitive, full employment outcomes,**
20) **disturbed and unscrupulous democratic representatives usurp the majority's will (and violate minority rights protection).**

In every instance, consumers', suppliers' and leaders' actions are disturbed. The term "disturbed" includes all psychological forces causing economic actors to deviate from the Pareto ideal including impractical instincts, passions, neuroses and psychoses.

In many instances distortions caused by disturbed psychological states are aggravated by unscrupulous motives; that is, all unethical behavior incompatible with Adam Smith's notion of moral duty and John Locke's concept of social contract.

Abnormal psychology and immorality explain why markets and plans in the neo-realist realm flagrantly deviate from the Paretian ideal. The distortions aren't merely due to Simon-type satisficing. They are attributable to psychological malfunctions and malign intentions. The first offers a psychological explanation; the second echoes the hoary conviction that humans are apt to sin.

Both explanations are plausible and readily confirmed by "being in the world." No one should be surprised that the Enlightenment faith in reason is overdrawn. However, the close correspondence between the neoclassical and neo-realist models is revealing. Individuals in both realms grapple with the same problems in similar ways, but generate drastically different outcomes: one Pareto efficient, the other often Pareto-esque. Reason enables neoclassical actors to realize their Pareto potential; aberrant psychology and unscrupulousness thwart it.

Neo-realist actors that pantomime rational utility-seekers, compute opportunity costs, form markets, and compete, but their motives and yardsticks are warped. They appear to rationally economize, but minimize and maximize the wrong things with pernicious results.

Authority

The correspondences between the neoclassical and neo-realist models also apply to sovereignty. In the neoclassical world, consumers rule. Their preferences determine supplies in the private and public sectors. The sovereigns in neo-realist dystopias are either disturbed and unscrupulous consumers or those who usurp power. Either way government will be Pareto inefficient and corrupt (in accordance with neo-realism's axioms). The neo-realist universe often offers a choice between lunatics ruling themselves, or delegating the task to disturbed and unscrupulous custodians. The contrast between Enlightenment and benighted government couldn't be starker, and provides deep insight into why reality as most people experience it bears little correspondence either to neoclassical idealism or neoclassical realism. Governance in the neo-realist realm isn't a simple matter of rational efficiency. It is the paradoxical consequence of disturbed and unprincipled leaders trying to persuade and coerce distressed and unscrupulous citizens to damage limit.

Prospects are grim, but only in varying degrees depending on prevailing mixes of ideal, realist and neo-realist forces. It can be plausibly supposed that the saner the society the brighter the outlook. However, assessments depend on the norms selected. People can legitimately find fault with Pareto optimal outcomes, and even find virtue in lunacy from a Bergsonian normative view point.

Varieties of Neo-realist Experience

Sigmund Freud's casting of the ego as an inept mediator between impractical hedonism and impractical conscience sheds valuable light on human misbehavior, exposing the psychological roots of economic pathologies like coercion, injustice, recklessness, dogmatism and crises. It reveals that neo-realist behavior may be the norm, rather than the exception, even before factoring in the possibilities of evil.

"Impractical instincts" including the urges to romanticize[4] and rationalize incline many to misbehave.[5] Weak egos are especially indulgent, and become licentious under psychological duress. They are easily intimidated by the emotional force of incensed ids bristling against repression. Threats disorient egos (neurosis and psychosis) and induce them to relent. Disturbed and unscrupulous self-seeking therefore isn't exceptional. Emotionally charged behavior comes with the Pareto-esque territory.[6]

---

[4]This may include martyrdom and altruism, although Paul Samuelson shows that altruism also may be "rational" within a neoclassical individualist utility framework. Paul Samuelson (November 1954). "The Pure Theory of Public Expenditure," *The Review of Economics and Statistics*, Vol. 36, No. 4, pp. 387–389. Stefano Zamagni (ed.) (1995). *The Economics of Altruism*, London: Edward Elgar. Gary Becker (1974). "A Theory of Social Interactions," *Journal of Political Economy*, Vol. 82, No. 6, pp. 106–1093.

[5]Keynes and Joan Robinson use the term "animal spirits" to describe entrepreneurial vigor. The phenomenon reflects an id driven "impractical" urge with a happy ending. See Joan Robinson (1962). *Economic Philosophy*, London: C.A. Watts.

[6]The power of these strategies depends on the degree to which minds can scientifically formulate utilitarian cause and effect, and on peoples' willingness to be realistic. Charles Sanders Peirce called this no nonsense scientific approach to discovering knowledge the "pragmatic method." He famously advised scientists to economize their effort by avoiding daydreaming and choosing the most promising hypotheses, and devised standards for evaluating the likelihood that any hypothesis would be scientifically fruitful.

His advice proved to be effective in laboratory research, but more difficult to apply in people's private lives. Desires and anxieties frequently trump pragmatic experimentation with outcomes depending on the quality of reasoning in all categories and the weight the mind assigns across categories to (1) rational selection, (2) interior existence, (3) self-discovery, (4) therapy, and (5) consciousness-raising.

This decomposition allows us to conceptualize neo-realist "utility" seeking as a two level programming algorithm where the mind pursues diverse objectives according to specific rules in each category at the primal level (rational selection, musing, learning by doing, self-criticism, and heightened awareness), and then engages in a libido, ego, superego struggle for psychic time and energy (prioritization). Rational selectors at the primal level diligently search their opportunity sets, and suppress daydreaming. Self-discoverers are preoccupied with "being in the world." Neurotics are obsessed with their irrational concerns. Consciousness-raisers introspect, while at a higher level the ego arbitrates conflicting demands.

If emotional and discovery processes outlined above (categories 2–5) crowd out rational selection, economics withers because daydreamers, self-discoverers, self-criticizers and consciousness-raisers pay scant attention to utility possibilities and marginal costs. If emotion doesn't dominate in these same categories, then reason and the ego pragmatically fix priorities allowing people not only to economize in a perfunctory sense, but across the spectrum of their emotional, ethical, spiritual and psycho-economic needs.

Coercion and Injustice

The Philosophes believed in free choice. They opposed forced labor, extortive contracting, compulsory purchases, and coercive price and wage fixing. Contemporary monopoly and oligopoly theories address arms-length price manipulation, but usually disregard intimidation. This gives the impression that economic relations are arms-length and mostly competitive, an outlook incompatible with the dynamics of the human psyche.

Individuals and governments widely transgress the economic rights of others, often flagrantly. Slavery has been common place for millennia. The term is applied to a wide range of master-slave relationships where individuals and organizations compel others to involuntarily provide services. The compulsion may be applied with or without formal ownership rights, or state sanction.

Individual and social wellbeing depend on the exact state of play between these extremes; that is, on the power and rational quality of each pragmatically informed psycho-economic aspect. Pragmatism isn't a panacea; nonetheless, it provides a superior framework for parsing the utilitarian effects of omitted variables without discarding the insights provided by optimization and satisficing theory.

It displaces harmonious rational utility seeking as the sole cause of human behavior without denying its legitimate role and encourages analysts to anticipate how and why other psychological factors may falsify standard behavioral expectations with or without just cause.

Moreover, reflection suggests that the process of multi-dimensional psycho-economic "utility seeking" has affinities with rational selection. The principle of diminishing returns applies to some extent in each psychological category. The pleasures of daydreaming, self-discovering, self-criticism, and consciousness-raising are apt to wane as each activity continues until people find that they prefer switching to something else. They are likely to adapt to shifting circumstances including changing price signals just like pure rational selectors.

This navigational mechanism (marginal utilities and prices) doesn't come to the same thing as rational selection because reason guided utility seeking is spotty. Nonetheless, rational management does tend to propel people from inferior to self-perceived improved states in fits and starts, providing a plausible explanation for how they lose and find their bearings. The prospect is less grandiose than Pareto bliss, but much more realistic, and wholly consistent with Herbert Simon's bounded rationality findings investigated in Chapter 3. *Pragmatism as a Principle and Method of Right Thinking: the 1903 Harvard Lectures on Pragmatism by Charles Sanders Peirc*e. Edited by Patricia Ann Turrisi (State University of New York Press, Albany, New York, 1997). *Reasoning and the Logic of Things: the Cambridge Conferences Lectures of 1898*. Edited by Kenneth Laine Ketner (Harvard University Press, Cambridge, Massachusetts, 1992).

Slavery is most often conceived as an extreme form of bondage where the weak are treated as freehold private property without human rights, forced to labor for their master's benefit. Slaves frequently were captured foes compelled to work in the fields and on construction projects (pharaonic Egypt), but they also were private and state owned industrial serfs forced to work without pay (19th century Russia).[7]

Slave regimes aren't uniformly harsh. President Thomas Jefferson's slaves were permitted to work for their own account after hours and own personal property.[8] Cultural attitudes likewise sometimes provided slaves with limited protections.

The essential characteristic of proprietary slavery is its violation of the Philosophes' premise that humans everywhere possess equal rights, protections and opportunities. Bondage impairs slaves' ability to rationally select, optimize and manage their utility; *ipso facto*, reducing their utility possibilities.

The same principle holds for non-proprietary bondage where "masters" have the power to coerce weak parties to provide services against their will. This category includes indentured servitude, company unions, impressment, military conscription, forced labor (Nazi concentration camps and Soviet Gulag), and various kinds of "sexual slavery." The Rome Statute of the International Court of Justice classifies many of these abuses as "crimes against humanity,"[9] but they persist nonetheless.

---

[7]Alexander Gerschenkron (1962). "Russia: Patterns and Problems of Economic Development, 1861–1958," in Gerschenkron (ed.), *Economic Backwardness in Historical Perspective*, Cambridge, MA: Harvard University Press, pp. 119–151.

[8]Henry Wiencek (2012). *Master of the Mountain: Thomas Jefferson and His Slaves*, New York: Farrar, Strauss & Giroux.

[9]**Article 7: Crimes against humanity**

1. For the purpose of this Statute, "crime against humanity" means any of the following acts when committed as part of a widespread or systematic attack directed against any civilian population, with knowledge of the attack:

   (a) Murder;
   (b) Extermination;
   (c) Enslavement;
   (d) Deportation or forcible transfer of population;
   (e) Imprisonment or other severe deprivation of physical liberty in violation of fundamental rules of international law;

Violence and intimidation also play large roles in organized crime: gambling, prostitution, pornography, money laundering, drug and cigarette trafficking, piracy, poaching, environmental despoliation, counterfeiting, identity theft, extortion and the protection racket. It also is openly employed in un-organized crime of similar kinds among consumers, businesses and governments.

The urge to defy the ego's rules (rational, Enlightenment inspired laws) takes surreptitious forms too. People, businesses and governments deceive, defame, cheat, misrepresent, evade, pilfer, misappropriate, embezzle, defraud, steal and conspire (monopoly, oligopoly, and insider trading). They may "rationally select," and rationalize their misconduct, but this doesn't negate victims' pain and suffering.

Excessive demands for gratifications can be advanced as well through special pleadings; that is, unwarranted claims for privileges and entitlements. This includes exemptions, mandates, sinecures, hiring quotas, contract set-asides, regulations and perks written almost invisibly into the tax code for specific individuals and institutions; generic benefits of the same kinds for sectors of business, investors, NGOs, "charities," trade unions, workers, veterans, retirees, women, homosexuals and "deserving" minorities. All violate the Enlightenment competitive equal opportunity ethic whenever claims for special treatment aren't compelling. Most people's (ids) rightly or wrongly feel aggrieved (outraged), but this seldom justifies requiring the public to pay compensation.

Powerful ids are the enemies of rational selection, reason and social justice. They impel domineering and unscrupulous people to acquire

---

(f) Torture;

(g) Rape, sexual slavery, enforced prostitution, forced pregnancy, enforced sterilization, or any other form of sexual violence of comparable gravity;

(h) Persecution against any identifiable group or collectivity on political, racial, national, ethnic, cultural, religious, gender as defined in paragraph 3, or other grounds that are universally recognized as impermissible under international law, in connection with any act referred to in this paragraph or any crime within the jurisdiction of the Court;

(i) Enforced disappearance of persons;

(j) The crime of apartheid;

(k) Other inhumane acts of a similar character intentionally causing great suffering, or serious injury to body or to mental or physical health.

unearned income and wealth at the community's expense, often intensifying skill based competitive inequalities.

Recklessness

Unbridled passions combined with a callous disregard for collateral damage manifest themselves diversely. One particularly destructive form is speculative bubbles. Some people driven by greed go berserk, sweeping away prudence and responsibility. Others try to profit by fanning the flames, or free riding. The failure of reason (consistent choice, or judicious assessment) is wryly conveyed by the title of Carmen Reinhart's and Kenneth Rogoff's treatise: *This Time Will be Different: Eight Centuries of Financial Folly.*[10] Individuals and governments know from hard experience that speculative bubbles always end badly. They resolve to prevent recurrences by learning from past mistakes, yet in the neo-realist realm never do.

The lapse is partially explained by difficulties of prediction,[11] and the gains reaped by those nimble or powerful enough to win.[12] Blame also can be laid at the doorstep of human foibles (Reinhart's and Rogoff's "folly"), evil, and wishful thinking, but the true explanation often runs deeper. In the neo-realist realm, speculative bubbles may be primarily attributable to speculative machinations and "manias;" where psycho-pathologies sweep reason aside.

Dogmatism

The same principle applies to dogmatism in all its manifestations.[13] Individuals and institutions often govern themselves with guidelines and doctrines

---

[10]Carmen Rheinhart and Kenneth Rogoff (2009). *This Time Will be Different: Eight Centuries of Financial Folly*, Princeton, NJ: Princeton University Press.

[11]Torbjorn Becker (2012). "Prevention and Counter-measures," in Steven Rosefielde, Masaaki Kuboniwa and Satoshi Mizobata (eds.), *Prevention and Crisis Management: Lessons for Asia from the 2008 Crisis*, Singapore: World Scientific.

[12]Steven Rosefielde and Quinn Mills (2014). *Democracy and Its Elected Enemies*, Cambridge: Cambridge University Press, Chapter 8.

[13]*Dogma* (opinion in Greek) is the shared faith based doctrine of individuals, institutions, cultures, ideologies and religions. It cannot be changed or discarded without altering the foundations of the belief system.

tailored to suit ids rather than dispassionate reason. They invariably claim the moral high ground to ward off rivals, and make a pretense of flexibility, but rarely make significant concessions unless compelled to do so.

The dogma of full employment provides an instructive example. Self-professed believers in statist paradigms of the good society contend that full employment is essential and can be secured without damage by deftly crafting monetary, fiscal and regulatory policies fostering excess aggregate effective demand. They take the position that full employment can be achieved with a combination of optimal deficit spending (Fisherian concept) and a target inflation rate of 2%. When the dogma is falsified and exposed as delusory,[14] like all good dogmatists they simply up the ante demanding more deficit spending and monetary expansion (printing money). The dogma's text is a series of baseless contentions about goals and capabilities. Its subtext is the gratification of the ids inappropriate desires.

Collapse

Frenzy and *dogma* sometimes culminate in breakdowns and collapse. When ids run amok,[15] egos often become paralyzed, unable to cope with the stress and futility of rationally managing. People with paralyzed egos become catatonic and shutdown, remaining in vegetative states until the mind subconsciously adapts and reconstitutes itself on manageable terms. Catatonic men and women cannot rationally select or judiciously reason and must endure whatever happens until they gradually recover.

The same phenomenon collectively applies to groups, institutions, societies and nations. If all individuals go berserk or if a sufficient number behave this way, then national economies can suffer nervous breakdowns.

---

[14]A delusion is a false belief that is maintained despite compelling counter-evidence. It is akin to the pretensions discussed in Chapter 13, and may arise through the imaginative processes people employ to grasp reality. The degree to which delusions impair preference formation and thereby cause "pseudo-rational" utility optimizing and satisficing depends on their extent and tenacity. Persistent delusions that strongly reduce utility or are harmful are considered pathological and further challenge the Philosophes' faith in the invincible powers of reason.

[15]Jonathan Swift (1726). *Gulliver's Travels*. A yahoo is a crude, rude and obscenely coarse member of a race of brutes who embody all human vices.

Mild cases are called recessions; extreme ones hyper-depressions or "black swans."[16]

The collapse of the Russian economy 1989–1996 illustrates the black swan possibility. The Soviet Union's didn't tranquilly morph into democratic free enterprise Russia as Enlightenment rationalists confidently forecast.[17] Mikhail Gorbachev and Boris Yeltsin were incapable of coping with the libidinal forces released by their misconceived reforms and ceased effectively governing. Their "leader ego" paralysis catastrophically disordered the national economy causing GDP to plummet as much as 50%.[18]

The ongoing crisis in the European Union (EU) provides an interesting example of milder catatonia.[19] EU leaders misguided by their superegos talked themselves into constructing a dysfunctional supranational regime and cannot rouse themselves sufficiently to restore a healthier balance.[20]

Optimizing and satisficing utilitarian theories offer rival explanations for recessions, depressions, hyper-depressions and national economic collapse. They contain partial truths. However, just as in the case of speculative bubbles, aberrant psychology completes the picture.[21] The Soviet Union's collapse and many severe economic crises don't really make much sense if frenzy and incapacitated egos are excluded.

Legitimacy and Ideocracy

Aberrant behavior is routinely addressed with mental health initiatives and criminal sanctions, but the battle is seldom won because the inmates are

---

[16]Nassim Taleb (2007). *The Black Swan: The Impact of the Highly Improbable*, New York: Random House.

[17]Anders Aslund (2007). *Russia's Capitalist Revolution: Why Market Reform Succeeded and Democracy Failed*, Washington DC: Peterson Institute; Aslund (1995). *Building Capitalism: The Transformation of the Former Soviet Bloc* (Cambridge University Press, 2001), *How Russia Became a Market Economy*, Washington DC: Brookings.

[18]Steven Rosefielde and Stefan Hedlund, *Russia Since 1980: Wrestling With Westernization*, Cambridge UP, 2008.

[19]Assaf Razin and Steven Rosefielde (2012). "A Tale of a Politically-Failing Single-Currency Area," *Israel Economic Review*, Vol. 10, No. 1, pp. 125–138.

[20]Steven Rosefielde and Assaf Razin (December 2012). "What Really Ails the Eurozone?: Faulty Supranational Architecture," *Contemporary Economics*, No. 4.

[21]Garry Shiller (2005). *Irrational Exuberance*, Princeton NJ: Princeton University Press.

running the asylum. Disturbed and unscrupulous leaders often are able to pull the wool over the public's eyes by crafting persuasive narratives justifying their rule. The right to rule achieved by persuasion rather than compulsion is called legitimacy.[22] This can be accomplished as Max Weber suggests diversely through charismatic, traditional, rational-legal authority, or some combination of these three elements.[23]

There are innumerable subcategories of authoritarian and faux democratic regimes that claim to be "legitimate" because they have beguiled society into embracing their credos or charismatic ideas. Martin Malia calls them "ideocracies;" that is, systems governed by ideas and ideals, including neoclassical idealism and realism. They are almost invariably dangerous to individual and social welfare insofar as people are beguiled, rather than dispassionately convinced. Ideocracy provides a benevolent face masking hidden agendas of disturbed and unscrupulous insiders that illuminates why bad government is more the rule, than the exception. In the idealist universe, governments are compelled by reason to do the right thing. Leaders always make wise public choices. In the neo-realist world, prodding leaders to act wisely for the general good is a ceaseless struggle.

Contemporary sovereigns of all description who pursue their disturbed notions of self-interest rather than acting as passive popular agents in sane societies pull out all the stops to preserve, expand and sustain their political legitimacy. Ideocrats cunningly manipulate the media, cultural organizations, education, religious institutions, trade unions, law, bureaucracies, regulatory agencies, judiciaries, legislatures, presidencies, and markets domestically, and exert influence beyond national borders[24] The results of their efforts are always imperfect. Disturbed and unscrupulous sovereigns cannot optimize their personal utility because they refuse to

---

[22]Robert Dahl (1971). *Polyarchy: Participation and Opposition*, New Haven: Yale University Press. Seymore Lipset (1983). *Political Man: The Social Bases of Politics*, London: Heinemann. Carl Schmitt (2004). *Legality and Legitimacy*, Durham NC: Duke University Press. Legitimacy is the term used by political scientists to describe popular acceptance of governmental authority, including law. The concept can be extended to regimes where people acknowledge and acquiesce to authority without approval or consent.

[23]Max Weber (1978). *Economy and Society*, Berkeley CA: University of California Press.

[24]The process resembles a continuous, managed collective dialogue where people are conditioned to accept the sovereign axioms.

play by competitive neoclassical rules, perfect planning is unattainable, and their ideocracies are morally illegitimate from an Enlightenment perspective. Extreme cases include Hitler's racist "national socialism," and Pol Pot's surreal "terror communism" which exterminated more than 20% of the Cambodian people.[25] Nonetheless, bad ideocracies too often are successful, enabling morally illegitimate sovereigns to "legitimately" rule in enough eyes to sustain their power at the expense of good government and unfettered competition.

---

[25] Steven Rosefielde (2010). *Red Holocaust*, New York: Routledge.

Chapter 13

Opportunities

Neo-realist theory has another face. It includes a variety of utility and welfare enhancing behaviors overlooked by Enlightenment advocates of individual reason and freedom which require people to shun materialist utility maximizing, or adopt satisficing conventions that restrict or eliminate free individual choice for the greater good whenever public policy fails.[1] The first lacunae is exemplified by Theravada Buddhism; the second by Japanese communalist obligation.[2] This chapter examines both phenomena to substantiate the claim that the design of superior economic systems should not be restricted to idealist and realist neoclassical paradigms.

---

[1]There is nothing in the Enlightenment concept of reason that requires people to autonomously optimize or to be materialistic, spiritually insensitive, self-centered, ruthless, greedy, uncooperative and unsociable, either privately or in the public domain. Rational people not only are free to act collectively, mutually support each other (worker managed economies), they can merge their identities with others, live shared existences and devote themselves to spiritual pursuits unconcerned about income maximizing, economic growth and the accumulation of wealth. Most issues involving "higher callings" including the pursuit of renaissance humanist ideals, higher consciousness, and transcendence therefore can be incorporated within the idealist and realist neoclassical rubrics, but not all. Martin Weitzman (1986). *The Share Economy: Conquering Stagflation*, Cambridge MA: Harvard University Press.

[2]There is a fundamental distinction between collective and communal action. Collectivists cooperate to achieve better personal utilitarian outcomes, judged from each collective member's autonomous utility function. Communalists don't differentiate their private from the group's utility and operate with shared consciousness.

Nirvana

Theravada Buddhism views mundane desires including a comfortable life, shallow contentment and secular fulfillment as the cause of suffering and impediments to spiritual progress. They are lower neoclassical callings. The higher calling is harmony and transcendence in this life and across cycles of reincarnation (Samsara) until enlightened individuals attain nirvana.

This neo-realist Thervadin paradigm is codified by the FOUR NOBLE TRUTHS, and THE EIGHTFOLD PATH.[3] The FOUR NOBLE TRUTHS succinctly characterize the human predicament; the EIGHTFOLD PATH provides a roadmap to salvation. Theravadins assert that the primary noble truth is suffering (*dukkha*), arising from birth, aging, diseases, death, pain, love, and hate; as well as the impermanence of things people cherish. Suffering is partly physical, but primarily the mental and spiritual distress felt by unenlightened souls who cannot comprehend the human condition. The underlying cause of suffering (*dukkha samudaya*) is desire (both innocent and sinful) which leads to attachments and bondage including yearning for immortality. People cannot face their own mutability. Although they have no fixed, unchanging identity (*Anatta*; not self or permanent essence), western utilitarians in the Theravadin view make the illusory self the center of their reality. Their physical form, feelings, perceptions, cognitive structures and consciousness change moment by moment, yet many people persuade themselves that their essence (soul) is eternal.

The third noble truth is the good news that salvation exists (*dukkha nirodha*), even though it is futile to pursue permanence in this life. Suffering can be conquered by accepting the immutable transcendental truth of Theravada Buddhism.[4] The fourth noble truth is that freedom lies in following the Noble Eightfold Path, until the enlightened are freed from the cycle of rebirth.

---

[3]Theravada Buddhists believe that transience is eternal; that there never was, nor will be beginnings and ends of time. Aristotle, among others in the western tradition, take the opposite stance. Their analysis begins with the "unmoved prime mover," that is, an existence before change. On western theories of perception see John Locke (1689). *An Essay Concerning Human Understanding.* Rene Descartes (1641). *Meditations on First Philosophy.*

[4]It isn't clear to the author whether physical laws like gravity or the speed of light are fixed or mutable in Theravadin doctrine. Transcendental truths may be immutable.

The Noble Eightfold Path is the fourth Noble Truth, and is known as the Middle Way, represented by the dharma wheel. It has three divisions: wisdom, ethical conduct and concentration. Wisdom lies in acknowledging the immutable truth of Buddhism (1) holding the right view, and having the (2) right intention to act accordingly. Ethical conduct requires shunning activities incompatible with the right view, namely (3) wrong speech (lies including those people tell themselves), (4) wrong action (evil deeds like killing, stealing, despoiling nature) and (5) wrong occupation (evil occupations like prostitution and racketeering). Enlightened beings shun harming others, are respectful and compassionate.[5] Once wisdom and ethical conduct are assured, then attaining enlightenment only requires concentration: (6) right effort, (7) right mindfulness, and (8) right concentration. Adherence to the Noble Eightfold Path enlightens souls with knowledge that ultimately allows them to be extinguished and mysteriously absorbed into the eternal cosmic spirit.[6]

---

[5]The utility potential of wisely managed minds can be conceived as a Pareto ideal where the psyche is free from impractical instincts, precepts and neurosis, supplemented by the value added of intuition, imagination, self-discovery, self-criticism, higher consciousness and transcendence. Rational selection and the invisible hand incline individuals toward their potential, but require pragmatic assistance from critical reason and intuition. The role assigned to critical reason is paramount. People must discover themselves, devise congruent values, construct context, and hone their appreciative faculties to take full advantage of external opportunities. Pragmatism and critical reason facilitate this by scientifically identifying connectives; distinguishing art from artifice, and truth from verisimilitude. They provide fallible, but useful tools for successfully navigating the world of illusion.[5] Erich Fromm (1992). *The Revision of Psychoanalysis*, Colorado: Westview Press. Erich Fromm, D.T. Suzuki and Richard De Martino (1960). *Zen Buddhism and Psychoanalysis*, Harper Colophon Books, New York. Erich Fromm (1967). *Socialist Humanism*, London: Allen Lane/Penguin Press. The search for higher states of individual utilitarian attainment converges in the limit to a fully conscious version of Pareto optimality where rational selectors maximize "critically reasoned" utilities. Psychoanalysis and psychiatry don't matter in this comprehensively humanized variant of the Pareto ideal, and it can be inferred that people are as subjectively well off as they can be.

[6]A fully enlightened person who is not yet the Buddha of our time is called an Arahant. He/she has eradicated the ten hindrances to enlightenment: (1) belief in a permanent personality (ego), (2) doubt (destructive skepticism), (3) attachment to rites, rituals, and ceremonies, (4) attachment to sense desires, (5) ill-will and anger, (6) craving for existence in the Form world (earth), (7) craving for existence in the Formless world (heavenly realms), (8) conceit, (9) restlessness, (10) ignorance.

The protocol (which has affinities with early Christian doctrine and Karl Marx's utopian communism) has nothing whatsoever to do with psychological self-discovery (true self),[7] identity, self-actualization, materialist desires, neoclassical utility optimizing or satisficing. The only thing that counts is self-disciplined purification of the mind on the pathway to nirvana. Theravada Buddhists contend that they are individually and collectively better off focusing on attaining enlightenment than by pursuing self-realization, affluence, or cost minimizing.

The neoclassical and Theravadin paradigms can be combined requiring Buddhists to jointly optimize the benefits of "awakening" and material success, but most Theravadins consider the option tainted.

Communal Adaptation

The Japanese reject Enlightenment individual self-seeking and unfettered competition. They don't utility or profit maximize, having been acculturated instead to defer to group authority for at least twenty five hundred years. People are taught from the cradle that it is shameful (not criminal) to avoid their obligations to family, community, company, government authorities and the emperor. This means that when conflicts arise between personal and group preference everyone is expected not only to acquiesce, but to embrace group values.[8] Group members who don't get their way are supposed to adjust their attitudes, instead of harboring resentments and passively resisting. People are permitted to have their say. The Japanese have

---

[7]The importance of personal psychology in the west distinguishes it from enlightenment seeking in the east. The humanist tradition sets actualizing every individual's potential as the highest good. People are supposed to cultivate their sensibilities and taste. The humanist search from a Theravadin perspective however is just another ego based delusion. It isn't self-actualization that matters. What counts is wisdom and compassion as guides to supreme enlightenment.

[8]Communal adaptation may not be the only reason that some individuals conform by voluntarily adjusting their preferences. They may doff a persona (mask) that fits their role, and sometimes confuse it with their anima. See Carl Jung (1972). *Two Essays on Analytical Psychology*, Princeton NJ: Princeton University Press. Regarding higher callings, anytime people devote themselves to causes and in the process disregard optimizing and realist satisficing, their behavior accords with neo-realist principles. Likewise, all mystically driven behavior is neo-realist.

elaborate cultural institutions fostering consensus building. However, once the group's decision is made, it becomes every individual's preference.[9]

This suggests from a neoclassical perspective that the Japanese economic system is inferior because communal culture obligates autonomous individuals to forego Pareto superior outcomes. The Japanese themselves disagree. They understand the sacrifice, however believe that it enhances, rather than diminishes their wellbeing (physical and mental health that provides a sound foundation for fulfillment and contentment).

The same attitude is taken toward a host of other anti-competitive "distortions" like employment for life which ostensibly degrades neoclassical economic efficiency, but from Masahiko Aoki's perspective provides "economies of trust" that enhance rather than diminish the quality of Japanese existence.[10] Communalism's higher calling in Aoki's eyes makes Japanese life superior to its autonomous individual utility seeking neoclassical rival. A similar argument can be made for Confucianism.[11]

Neo-realism versus Neoclassical Realism

The opportunities that neo-realist economics offer individuals and societies for enhancing wellbeing aren't included or are only inadequately incorporated in the neoclassical toolbox. They are substitutes for neoclassical economics or complements for enhancing Pareto welfare. Theravada Buddhism places little or no positive value on market competition or planning, while Japanese communalism is accommodative. It doesn't shun markets, it just subordinates business to the higher cause of obligated communal satisficing.

Both are part of the reality that Reinhart Selten correctly contends is missing in idealist neoclassical theory when he declared that "I am convinced of the need of reconstructing microeconomics on the basis of a

---

[9]Steven Rosefielde (2013). *Asian Economic Systems*, Singapore: World Scientific Publishers.

[10]Masahiko Aoki (2001). *Information, Incentives and Bargaining in the Japanese Economy*, Oxford: Oxford University Press.

[11]Young-oak Kim and Jung-kyu Kim (2013). *The Great Equal Society: Confucianism, China and the 21st Century*, Singapore: World Scientific.

more realistic picture of economic decision making,"[12] but they probably lie outside the scope of what he had in mind. His realist quest for a more scientific neoclassical economic theory rests primarily on the sensible desire of discovering a few first principles that can be used to explain all economic behavior. The complexity, contradictions and adaptability of human motivation and behavior however make this quest futile, and worse still counterproductive to the extent that they prevent economists from designing inclusively best systems and policies.

[12]Reinhard Selten (2002). "What is Bounded Rationality?" in Gerd Gigerenzer and Reinhard Selten (eds.), *Bounded Rationality: The Adaptive Tool Box*, Cambridge: MIT Press, pp. 13–36.

Part III

Inclusive Economics

Chapter 14

Umbrella of Complementary Paradigms

Economic behavior cannot be completely explained by rational utility-seeking principles. Individual and collective action may be governed by (1) Enlightenment rationality and values, (2) bounded rationality and satisficing, and (3) a host of other motivations excluded from the rational Enlightenment construct. All involve constrained choice theoretic strategies for utility improving utility based on rational, "rationalized," or emotional criteria.[1] None require people to choose wisely, even when they rationally select. Economic theory consequently is composed of linked complementary paradigms with some shared aspects, each distinguished by its own selective axioms. It necessarily constitutes an umbrella of complementary paradigms that only provides oblique insight into individual, societal and national wellbeing rather than a causally unified field theory of rational behavior and outcomes.

No paradigm is inherently true. The positive merit of each depends on causal accuracy. Normative merit depends on how individual observers assess outcomes for all three paradigms individually and the umbrella collectively.

The wellbeing (physical and mental health that provides a sound foundation for fulfillment and contentment) of individuals and societies accordingly is determined as a composite of individual and societal outcomes, assessed through diverse normative eyes. Nonetheless, a few generic

---

[1]Optimality theory relies wholly on reason. Realist satisficing and various neo-realist utility seeking employ mixed tools to assess comparative merit including heuristics.

139

observations can be made about the positive and normative merit of composite systems.

Economies that satisfy idealist neoclassical axioms possess the virtue of efficiency and Pareto optimality, and following Abram Bergson and James Meade can be responsive to collective concerns through optimal tax-transfers. They should also be macro-economically stable, grow optimally and can be given a socialist twist by invoking the programming duality between perfect competition and perfect planning. These features won't satisfy all critics, particularly egalitarians, but still offer an attractive package.

The principle objection to idealist neoclassical theoretic characterizations for both perfect markets and perfect plans is that they are false. Real market and planned economies are persistently marred by power (and consequently excess inequality), are inefficient and often macro-economically disordered.

Realist economic theory acknowledges these accusations, attributing the dysfunctions to bounded rationality and satisficing. Its descriptions and predictions correspond better with observed individual and national behavior, but still impart a patina of efficiency and second best Pareto merit that many consider unjustified.

Neo-realist theory opens an entirely different can of worms not just by attacking neoclassical assumptions and Pareto values, but through a frontal assault on Enlightenment axioms of rationality, virtue and motivation. Many of these criticisms were vetted during the Enlightenment and have been repeated and embellished thereafter by a wide range of theorists including Karl Marx and Sigmund Freud.[2] The essential message of neo-realist theory is twofold. First, the gulf separating neoclassical interpretations of economic performance and reality is mostly attributable to its failure to endogenize perverse anti-Enlightenment behaviors. Second, some types of behaviors excluded by Enlightenment principles including transcendental awareness and satisficing communality offer individuals and societies opportunities for enhancing wellbeing unattainable in pure neoclassical orders. When one or both of these alternatives is applicable,

---

[2]Sigmund Shlomo Freud (1930). *Civilization and its Discontents*, [*Das Unbehagen in der Kultur* ("The Uneasiness in Culture")].

neo-realist theories provide more accurate causal characterizations of economic action, and may offer a wider range of constructive policy options than their neoclassical rivals.

This however doesn't mean that neo-realism is comprehensively true and neoclassical theories are false. Individual and social behavior and corresponding policy options normally will be captured best by an admixture of the three complementary paradigms. The task of economic theory from the perspective of inclusive economics (umbrella of linked complementary paradigms) therefore is to accurately grasp complexities and devise appropriately targeted interventions tailored to reality instead of using the distorted lens of any single paradigm to interpret the whole.

Chapter 15

Truth

Inclusive economics is an ambiguous synthetic social science, despite its comprehensiveness, axiomatic versatility and conceptual rigor. Like other social sciences, its powers of prediction are weak, especially in the macro-economic domain. This is why Alexander Rosenberg dismisses idealist and realist neoclassical theoretic aspect of synthetic economic science as "mathematical politics."[1] Real science for him must be comprehensively falsifiable. The criterion however is too stringent. Logically sound, but weakly falsifiable neoclassical theories create weak forms of useful knowledge. They are weakly scientific and better than idle speculation.

The same principle holds for inclusive economic theory which if applied properly should prove more strongly falsifiable. Inclusive economic theory is more than conjecture, and is capable of providing better predictions than idealist or realist neoclassical theories in most circumstances. In Karl Popper's terminology, it offers truth-like verisimilitude, that is, broad insight into causes and effects. Inclusive economic theory likewise is compatible with Charles Sanders Peirce's concept of experimental science by

---

[1]Alexander Rosenberg (1994). *Mathematic Politics or Science of Diminishing Returns*, Chicago: University of Chicago Press. Alex Rosenberg and Tyler Curtain (August 24, 2013). "What is Economics Good For?" *The Stone*. Cf. Donald (Deidre) McCloskey (December 1993). Review of Alexander Rosenberg, Mathematic Politics or Science of Diminishing Returns, *The History of Science Society*, Vol. 84, No. 4, pp. 838–839. The philosophers of science are hostile to neoclassical theory and reject it as a science. Rosenberg and Curtain assert that "None of our models of science really fit economics at all."

144 *Inclusive Economic Theory*

providing a middle ground between anti-skepticism and fallibilism,[2] and can be combined with critical rationality to deconstruct rival interpretative claims.[3]

The Soviet economy offers an instructive example. During the late 1960s and 1970s, many mathematically inclined neoclassical theorists portrayed the USSR's command economy as a central planned system striving to achieve "computopia" by simulating competitive markets with linear programming and related incentive methods.[4] This created a presumption that the Soviet economy could achieve neoclassical potentials and its performance could be validly interpreted with neoclassical norms (Bergson's adjusted factor cost method).[5] Official Soviet statistics and

[2]*Pragmatism as a Principle and Method of Right Thinking: the 1903 Harvard Lectures on Pragmatism by Charles Sanders Peirce.* Edited by Patricia Ann Turrisi (State University of New York Press, Albany, New York, 1997). *Reasoning and the Logic of Things: the Cambridge Conferences Lectures of 1898.* Edited by Kenneth Laine Ketner (Harvard University Press, Cambridge, Massachusetts, 1992). Charles Sanders Peirce calls the willingness of people to be realist in the discovery of knowledge the "pragmatic method." He famously advised scientists to economize their effort by avoiding daydreaming and choosing the most promising hypotheses, and devised standards for evaluating the likelihood that any hypothesis would be scientifically fruitful. Fallibilism is a philosophical stance that justifies holding unproven principles pending further evidence. The middle ground between anti-skepticism and fallbilism is patchwork verification.

[3]Karl Popper (1962). *The Open Society and Its Enemies*, New York: Harper & Row. Popper (1985). "The Rationality Principle," in: David Miller (ed.) *Popper Selections*, Princeton: Princeton University Press. Jacques Derrida (1973). *Speech and Phenomena and Other Essays on Husserl's Theory of Signs*, Evanston: Northwestern UP.

[4]Dorfman, Robert, Paul Samuelson and Robert Solow (1958). *Linear Programming and Economic Analysis*, McGraw-Hill, New York. Dunlop, John and Nikolay Fedorenko (1969). *Planning and Markets: Modern Trends in Various Economic Systems*, McGraw Hill, New York. Ellman, Michael (1971). *Soviet Planning Today, Proposals for an Optimally Functioning Economic System*, Cambridge University Press. Fedorenko, Nikolay (1974). *Optimal Functioning System for a Socialist Economy*, Progress, Moscow. Egon Neuberger (March 1966). "Libermanism, Computopia, and the Visible Hand: The Question of Informational Efficiency," *American Economic Review*, Vol. 56, No. 1/2, pp. 131–144. Martin Weitzman (1970). "Iterative Multi-Level Planning with Production Targets," *Econometrica* Vol. 38, pp. 50–65. Martin Weitzman (1974). "Prices versus Quantities." *Review of Economic Studies*, Vol. 41, pp. 477–491.

[5]Steven Rosefielde and Ralph W. Pfouts (1998). "The Mis-specification of Soviet Production Potential: Adjusted Factor Costing and Bergson's Efficiency Standard," in Rosefielde (ed.), *Efficiency and Russia's Economic Recovery Potential to the Year 2000 and Beyond*, Ashgate, Aldershot, pp. 11–31.

western re-estimates seemed to corroborate the surmise. Soviet industrial and NMP growth during this period outpaced America and those of most west European nations.[6] Neoclassical prediction appeared to be econometrically verified.

Detailed scrutiny of Soviet institutions moreover confirmed that the system was comprehensively and rationally designed. The supply system had a clear input-output structure and supervisory chain of command. Information and planning systems were well established. Demand was determined by "systems directors," and supporting financial, banking, investment, price fixing, incentive setting, regulatory and disciplinary mechanisms were all in place. The Soviets apparently were rational men. Although they rejected private property, markets and entrepreneurship, nonetheless they found a viable way to efficiently operate their economy.[7] Neither Abram Bergson nor the CIA foresaw any possibility of Soviet economic collapse.[8]

The handwriting however had long been on the wall.[9] Everyone knew and acknowledged that Soviet planning was flawed,[10] but the imperfections were brushed aside as blemishes, rather than proof that the neoclassical paradigm fundamentally misrepresented the Soviet modus operandi.

[6]Steven Rosefielde (2007). *Russian Economy From Lenin to Putin*, New York: Wiley.

[7]Abram Bergson (1978). *Productivity and the Social System — The USSR and the West*, Harvard University Press, Cambridge, MA. Steven Rosefielde (1998), "Comparative Production Potential in the USSR and the West: Pre-Transition Assessments, in Rosefielde (ed.), *Efficiency and Russia's Economic Recovery Potential to the Year 2000 and Beyond*, Ashgate, Aldershot, London, pp. 101–135.

[8]Abram Bergson (1991). "The USSR Before the Fall: How Poor and Why?" *Journal of Economic Perspectives*, No. 5, Fall, pp. 29–44.

[9]Steven Rosefielde (1981). "Knowledge and Socialism," in Rosefielde (ed.), *Economic Welfare and the Economics of Soviet Socialism*, Cambridge UP, London, pp. 5–24. Steven Rosefielde (June 2005). "Tea Leaves and Productivity: Bergsonian Norms for Gauging the Soviet Future," *Comparative Economic Studies*, Vol. 47, No. 2, pp. 259–273. Steven Rosefielde (April 1988). "The Soviet Economy in Crisis: Birman's Cumulative Disequilibrium Hypothesis," *Soviet Studies*, Vol. XL, No. 1, pp. 222–244.

[10]Gregory Grossman, G. (1963). "Notes for a Theory of the Command Economy," *Soviet Studies*, Vol. 15, No. 2, 1963, pp. 101–123. Grossman (1977). "The 'Second Economy' of the USSR," *Problems of Communism*, Vol. 26, No. 5, pp. 25–40. Alec Nove (1977), *The Soviet Economic System*, London: George Allen and Unwin. Richard Ericson (March 2006). "Command Versus 'Shadow': The Conflicted Soul of the Soviet Economy," *Comparative Economic Studies*, Vol. 48, No. 1, pp. 50–76.

It wasn't taken seriously because there was no inclusive economic theory establishing that ideal and realistic neoclassical theories were merely components of economic theory under a broad umbrella of linked complementary paradigms. Had inclusive economic theory been devised earlier, neoclassical theorists would have recognized that they could not take Soviet claims of rational planning at face value and needed a tool immune from statistical falsification (with corrupt data) to confirm their hypotheses.[11] The Weberian concept of legitimation (ideocracy) would have alerted them to the possibility that Soviet power wasn't founded on optimizing principles, and critical rationality would have provided the missing tool for confirming the hypothesis.

Karl Popper's concept of critical rationality is a device for piercing semblances to ascertain whether ostensibly plausible claims can withstand close scrutiny. Its application begins by accepting the proposition that the Soviets desired optimal planning and took steps to construct an appropriate institutional apparatus. It then proceeds to investigate whether these institutions were capable of carrying out the mission. This task isn't difficult. The Soviets produced approximately 27 million distinct products annually, but only centrally planned 125. The gap was bridged by linear disaggregation without systems directors having any inkling about purchasers' preferences. The State Planning Agency (GOSPLAN) could run as many linear programs as it desired, but it could never adequately simulate a competitive market optimum, given either consumers or systems directors' preferences. The neoclassical presumption that the Soviet economic system operated on the same optimizing principles as competitive markets was a mirage. Rationality was too bounded to close the gap![12]

Further application of critical rationality reveals that Soviet production, given system directors' macro budgeting priorities, was determined by rule of thumb and a crazy quilt of effort mobilizing incentives.[13] As Igor Birman

---

[11] Steven Rosefielde (2003). "The Riddle of Postwar Soviet Economic Growth: Statistics Lied and Were Misconstrued," *Europe-Asia Studies*, Vol. 53, No. 3, pp. 469–481.

[12] Cf. Abram Bergson (1966). "Socialist Calculation: A Further Word," in Bergson, *Essays in Normative Economics*, Cambridge, MA: Harvard University Press, pp. 237–242.

[13] Joseph Berliner (1978). *The Innovation Decision in Soviet Industry*, Cambridge MA: MIT Press. Conn, David (September 1979). "A Comparison of Alternative Incentive Structures for Centrally Planned Economic Systems," *Journal of Comparative Economics*, Vol. 3, No. 3, pp. 235–253.

explained central plans were constructed "from the achieved level,"[14] and then cobbled together with information on factor supply prospects, neutral technological progress and political aspirations. The achieved level was real; the rest was mostly Mickey Mouse. Aggregate plans were compiled, disaggregated and affected production by constraining managerial resource access and providing guidance on supply assortments. Managers motivated by incentives and penalties produced whatever maximized their utility under prevailing constraints without regard to systems directors' micro-preferences and purchasers' demands.[15] The system worked in the sense that it mobilized resources and produced large and sometimes increasing supplies of goods few desired. The military flourished, and consumers barely survived in an economy of shortage.[16]

There would have been no reason for neoclassical Sovietologists to be surprised by the USSR's demise, if they had the opportunity to acquaint themselves with inclusive economic theory and science. Critical reason and truth-like verisimilitude don't establish the full truth, but they are much more powerful than arbitrary reliance of any single paradigm enclosed in the inclusive umbrella.[17]

Conclusion

A "unified field" theory of economics akin to physics is impossible because no plausible set of parsimonious axioms exist that adequately capture the diversity of human behavior.[18] It might seem that Paul Samuelson's method

---

[14]Igor Birman, Экономика недостач. Нью-Йорк: Chalidze publications, 1983.

[15]Steven Rosefiede and Ralph W. Pfouts (1995). "Economic Optimization and Technical Efficiency in Soviet Enterprises Jointly Regulated by Plans and Incentives," *European Economic Review*, Vol. 32, No. 6, pp. 1285–1299.

[16]Igor Birman (1983). Экономика недостач. Нью-Йорк: Chalidze publications.

[17]Further analysis taking historical factors into consideration would have revealed that the Soviet economic system was a variant of the "Muscovite paradigm," rooted in the governance principles of Ivan the Great and Ivan the Terrible. See Steven Rosefielde (2007). *Russian Economy From Lenin to Putin*, New York: Wiley.

[18]A unified field theory in physics refers to the possibility of incorporating all fundamental forces and elementary particles in a single field. The term was coined by Albert Einstein who sought to unify the general theory of relativity with electromagnetism. He failed, and no one else has succeeded.

of treating economics primarily as a form of mathematical physics,[19] combined with Herbert Simon's and Reinhart Selten's realist refinements and
normative public policy theory might point the way,[20] but once it is appreciated that people's behavior is co-determined by reason, rationalization, disturbed psychology, unscrupulousness, non-autonomous communal utility
seeking, and higher callings incompatible with Enlightenment premises the
hope becomes illusory. There isn't one universal explanation of economic
behavior based on a few key axioms. Instead there are three linked complementary paradigms and a myriad of subcases. Neoclassical economic
theory in both its ideal and realist forms constitutes the first two paradigms.
They serve admirably when core axioms hold, but otherwise are incomplete
and misleading. Neo-realist theory covers the rest of the territory, but its
assumptions are unmanageably heterogeneous and case specific. The three
linked paradigms together provide an inclusive economic theory offering
the prospect of weak knowledge and truth-like verisimilitude. Inclusive
economic theory as has been demonstrated can be very powerful. However
the umbrella isn't a unified theory in Albert Einstein's Olympian sense and
contradicts Selten's hope that a unified theory can be constructed on realist
neoclassical principles alone. Inclusive economic theory is a second best
akin to the coexistence of quantum physics and relativity.

When the assumptions of ideal neoclassical theory hold, they always
provide Pareto optimal solutions across space and time. When they don't

---

[19]Paul Samuelson (1947), *Foundations of Economic Analysis*, Cambridge: Harvard University Press. Samuelson was one of the first economists to generalize and apply mathematical
methods developed for the study of thermodynamics to economics. His *Foundations of
Economic Analysis* is based on the methods of American thermodynamicist Willard Gibbs,
specifically Gibbs' 1876 paper "On the Equilibrium of Heterogeneous Substances." See
Samuelson, "Gibbs in Economics," Proceedings of the Gibbs Symposium (Providence, RI),
1990, pp. 255–267. Samuelson also adopted the techniques of Henri Louis Le Chatelier
(Le Chatelier principle) in the *Foundations* to introduce comparative statics into economic
microtheory. See Joseph McCauley (2003). "Thermodynamic Analogies in Economics and
Finance: Instability of Markets," *Physica*, Vol. 329, pp. 199–212.

[20]Abram Bergson explained how this might be accomplished more than forty years ago.
See Abram Bergson (October 1976). "Social Choice and Welfare Economics Under Repre-
sentative government," *Journal of Economics*, Vol. 6, No. 3, 1976, pp. 171–190. Cf. Steven
Rosefielde (June 2005) "Tea Leaves and Productivity: Bergsonian Norms for Gauging the
Soviet Future," *Comparative Economic Studies*, Vol. 47, No. 2, pp. 259–273.

realist and neo-realist paradigms govern aspects of outcomes, and causalities can be revealed in whole or part by parsing theory and evidence with
critical rationality to identify truth-like verisimilitudes, "truths" that can
be evaluated further with Bergsonian welfare theory. Inclusive economic
theory consequently provides richer insight into causality than neoclassical
theory, even though it cannot resolve all disputes and paradoxes.

This has profound practical implications for public policy designed
to promote wellbeing. It means that over reliance on idealist and realist neoclassical microeconomic and macroeconomic theories must yield
inefficient and often counterproductive results whenever these paradigms
fail to adequately capture the pernicious effects of anticompetitive forces,
unscrupulousness, psychological aberrations, and opportunities for enhancing wellbeing outside the Pareto framework. The under productivity,
excessive unemployment, retarded economic growth, inequality, over
indebtedness, crises and other macroeconomic disorders besetting the
global economy today are strongly attributable to neoclassical myopia. An
inclusive theoretical framework that pairs policies issue by issue with the
right idealist neoclassical, realist neoclassical and neo-realist paradigms
will yield much better results.

Mathematical Appendices

Appendix 1

Bergsonian Social Welfare Functions

Abram Bergson demonstrated more than a half century ago that the virtue of any system can be calibrated with social welfare functions,[1] given the appraiser's scale of value. Algebraically,

$$W = F(U_1, U_2, U_3, U_n; x, y, z), \qquad (A1.1)$$

where,

$U_i =$ the utility of the ith individual derived from consumption and savings,

$x, y, z =$ relational determinants of utility such as civil liberties and equality,

$F =$ a value forming function aggregating individual utilities generated directly from consumption and indirectly from the relational variables.

The Bergsonian W can be a point estimate, or interpreted as a set of social welfare curves (iso-welfare), analogous to consumer iso-utility curves convex to the origin. If the highest attainable iso-welfare curve is tangent at E, then the west-utopian outcome is best not only from the standpoint of underlying Pareto optimizing axioms, but in terms of the

---

[1]Abram Bergson (1938). "A Reformulation of Certain Aspects of Welfare Economics," *Quarterly Journal of Economics*, Vol. 52, No. 1, pp. 310–334. Bergson (1954). "The Concept of Social Welfare," *Quarterly Journal of Economics*, Vol. 68, No. 2, pp. 233–253. Bergson (1976). "Social Choice Under Representative Government", *Journal of Public Economics*, Vol. 6, No. 3, pp. 171–190.

judge's norms. The relational variable (x) in Figure 2.4 is the distribution of utilities between the two participants.

The judge's notion of the best however need not coincide with point E. The highest tangency can lie at any point E^* along a utility possibilities frontier (UPF), derived from alternative retail distributions (including transfers) in Figure 2.3. Moreover, once the game is begun, constants like the initial wealth distribution can be transformed into variables, generating new sets of utility possibilities (the envelop of which is a grand utility possibilities frontier), so that point E which once provisionally seemed best becomes quite inferior from the judge's point of view. For example, some feminist's welfare forming function F may assign a very low weight to men's utility. This will make point E in Figure 2.4 immediately inferior (assuming one participant is male, the other female), and trigger a series of interactive adjustments of many complex kinds, that in the end yield a solution where men receive a bare minimum, while women consume the rest. This can be illustrated in the utility possibility space as an E point close to the axis of the female participant, and above a level attainable merely by redistributing the Pareto retail supply of goods in Figure 2.3.

Judges can compute Bergsonian Ws from ordinal or cardinal utility indicators. Cardinal measures are better because they yield exact interpersonally consistent magnitudes that can facilitate rational debate among rival judges. Alas, despite the probabilistic cardinal utility measurement techniques devised by John von Neumann and Oskar Morgenstern,[2] experience has shown that it is impossible to calculate credible Bersgsonian Ws fixing a unique and supreme social welfare optimum. Women may justifiably feel that men deserve little, but they cannot prove it with utility calculus.

---

[2]John von Neumann and Oskar Morgenstern (2007). *Theory of Games and Economic Behavior* (Commemorative Edition), Princeton: Princeton University Press.

Appendix 2

Idealist Neoclassical Consumer Utility Optimization

The theory of consumer behavior that is accepted by most economic theorists, is based on a mathematical process that is sometimes called "constrained optimization." This refers to maximizing or minimizing a mathematical function while the variables of the function are "constrained" or controlled by another function.

To show how this fits into economic theory we have to introduce the "utility function." This is a mathematical function that relates quantity of goods and services that a consumer consumes, to the utility that he derives from them. Thus, a utility function might be written as

$$u = \psi(x_1, x_2, \ldots, x_n). \tag{A2.1}$$

In this equation the xs represent the quantities of goods and services the consumer receives. Thus x_1 might be the amount of coffee he drinks, while x_2 might be a knit scarf, and x_{17} might be taxi rides, etc. Of course u represents the amount of utility. Hence, the utility function represented by ψ transforms the quantities of goods and services obtained into u, the amount of utility experienced by the consumer.

The amount of utility increases as the quantity of goods and services increases. Thus,

$$\frac{\partial u}{\partial x_j} > 0, \, (j = 1, \ldots, n). \tag{A2.2}$$

The derivative $\frac{\partial u}{\partial x_j}$, represents marginal utility. For convenience we will use subscripts to indicate differentiation, e.g., $\psi_i = \frac{\partial u}{\partial x_j}$.

Clearly the consumer wants to maximize his utility. But he is constrained in his maximization efforts by the amount of money that he can spend. He has a "budget constraint." This can be written as

$$M = \sum_{j=1}^{m} p_j x_i,$$

M represents his income. The p's represent the prices of the goods and services. So he wants to maximize (A2.2) while restraining the x's by the budget equation.

To do this, it is necessary to form an equation of this sort:

$$\varphi = \psi(x_1, \ldots, x_n) - \lambda \left(\sum_j p_j x_j - M \right). \qquad \text{(A2.3)}$$

Equations like (A2.3) are called Lagrangians after the mathematician Lagrange. If we maximize an equation like (A2.3) we are maximizing $\psi(\ )$ while constraining the variables by the budget equation. The symbol λ is called a Lagrange multiplier. Its role will be developed as the argument proceeds.

To find the constrained maximum of (A2.3), the first derivatives must be set equal to zero, hence

$$\varphi_j = \psi_j - \lambda p_j = 0, \ (j = 1, \ldots, n),$$
$$\varphi_\lambda = \sum_j p_j x_j - M = 0. \qquad \text{(A2.4)}$$

These $n + 1$ first order or first derivative equations must hold.

To insure that we have a maximum; not a minimum, additional conditions must hold on the second derivatives. The conditions are that the determinant

$$\begin{vmatrix} \psi_{11} & \cdots\cdots\cdots & \psi_n p_1 \\ \psi_{21} & \cdots\cdots\cdots & \psi_{2n} p_2 \\ \psi_{n1} & \cdots\cdots\cdots & \psi_{nn} p_n \\ p_1, & \cdots\cdots\cdots & p_n 0 \end{vmatrix}$$

must have nested, bordered minors that alternate in sign, thus

$$\begin{vmatrix} \psi_{11} & \psi_{12} & \psi_{13} & p_1 \\ \psi_{21} & \psi_{22} & \psi_{23} & p_2 \\ \psi_{31} & \psi_{32} & \psi_{33} & p_3 \\ p_1 & p_2 & p_3 & 0 \end{vmatrix} > 0,$$

$$\begin{vmatrix} \psi_{11} & \psi_{12} & \psi_{13} & \psi_{14} & p_1 \\ \psi_{21} & \psi_{22} & \psi_{23} & \psi_{24} & p_2 \\ \psi_{31} & \psi_{32} & \psi_{33} & \psi_{34} & p_3 \\ \psi_{41} & \psi_{42} & \psi_{43} & \psi_{44} & p_4 \\ p_1 & p_2 & p_3 & p_4 & 0 \end{vmatrix} < 0 \text{ etc.}$$

From (A2.4) we can get

$$\frac{\psi_1}{p_1} = \frac{\psi_2}{p_2} = \cdots = \frac{\psi_n}{p_n} = \lambda.$$

These equations show that in equilibrium the marginal utility per dollar must be the same for all goods. This is the usual textbook condition.

We could go on and derive the Slutsky substitution effect and income effect, but that is not necessary for our purpose.

Constrained optimization is the general case of which indifference curves, etc., are a special case. It is the pride of the economic theory of consumer behavior. We want to show that it is not realistic.

First we observe that it all depends on a utility function, a mathematical function that relates goods and services to a quantitative subjective scale of utility. Do you have a utility function? The writers do not have utility functions; nor, did anyone that they asked.

If nobody has a utility function, why are we using it as the basis of the theory of consumer behavior?

Have you ever seen a lady standing in a store, hurriedly evaluating a determinant to be sure she has a maximum, not a minimum? No? Neither have we.

Appendix 3

Idealist Neoclassical Production: Multiproduct Firm

Up to this point, we have not discussed the production of goods and services. We have alluded to production, but we have not examined it as an economic process. We have alluded to farming, manufacturing, and transporting goods, but we have not examined these various processes. Yet, they are fundamental. If goods were not manufactured and transported, each family would have to manufacture the goods they used which means it would be necessary to transport raw material into the area controlled by the family. Living standard would fall a great deal.

Manufacturing firms usually produce a number of similar goods. A firm or even a single factory that produces only one good is unusual. Producing sets of goods, often related goods, is common.

We use Z_{it} to indicate the amount of fixed factor t used in the production of product i. We use Z_t the available amount or we might say the total amount of fixed factor Z_t. We could write $\sum_i Z_{it} - Z_t \leq 0$. If all the fixed factor has been used, the equality will hold. If some of it is still available, the inequality will hold.

Each type of product that is manufactured in this factory gives rise to a "product function" which shows the relation between the use of factory input of fixed productive factors and variable productive factors. Hence, the "production function" for each product would appear as

$$x_i = f_i(y_{i1}, \ldots, y_{im}, z_{i1}, \ldots, z_{is})$$

$$i = 1, \ldots, n.$$

159

In a firm that produces more than one product, the problems of transferring fixed factors from use in producing one product to producing a different product arises. These transfers involve costs. These costs are indicated by the cost of transferring a small amount of fixed factor j

$$K = K(z_{11}, \ldots, z_{nz}),$$

to the production of product i. In addition, it may be said that the derivatives represent the costs of transferring fixed factors when the firm's structure changes due to a change of a parameter in the firm's cost structure. These changes are interesting because they are caused by parametric variation. A more complete discussion is provided elsewhere.[1]

The firm's cost minimization problem is that of minimizing all costs for a specified product mixture. Using F to designate fixed costs, we must note the costs for various kinds and levels of output.

Let us begin with the simplest case. The first produces only one good; it never produces any other product. This is the simplest case. In this case, there are fixed costs which we designate as F and various productive factors are used, including labor, materials, and others. To vary the firm's outputs, the quantities of these elements are varied.

We can write the firm's Lagrangian as

$$L = \sum_{i=1}^{n} \sum_{j=1}^{m} w_j \, y_{ij} + K(Z_{n1}, \ldots, Z_{ms}) + F$$

$$- \sum_{i=1}^{n} \lambda_i (f_i - x_i) - \sum_{r=1}^{s} \mu_r \left(\sum_{i=1}^{n} z_{ir} - Z_r \right). \qquad \text{(A3.1)}$$

Here, w_j, x_i, and Z_r are parameters and y_{ij}, z_{ir}, x_i, $\mu_r \geqq 0$ for all values of the indices.

The cost relationships that we will investigate are those arising from the parameters in (A3.1).

---

[1] Ralph W. Pfouts (1961). "The Theory of Cost and Production in the Multi-Product Firm," *Econometrica*, Vol. 29, pp. 650–658.

The easiest way to proceed is to begin by stating and proving two theorems on parametric variations in Lagrangian expressions. These theorems may then be applied to cost relationships in multiproduct form.

Consider a Lagrangian,

$$L^* = f(\zeta_1, \ldots, \zeta_m, \beta_1, \ldots, \beta_n) - \sum_l \rho_i g_i(\zeta_1, \ldots, \zeta_m, \alpha_i), \quad \text{(A3.2)}$$

in which the α and β are parameters.

In addition, we have

$$g_i(\zeta_1, \ldots, \zeta_m, \alpha_i) \leqq 0, \quad \text{(A3.3a)}$$

and

$$-\frac{\partial g_i}{\partial \alpha_t} = \delta_{it}. \quad \text{(A3.3b)}$$

The last notation is the Kronecker delta.

The effect of a small increase of α_i on the Langrangian (A3.2) may be shown as

$$\frac{\partial L^*}{\partial \alpha_t} = \sum_i \left[\frac{\partial f}{\partial \zeta_i} - \sum_i \rho_i \frac{\partial g_i}{\partial \zeta_i} \right] \frac{\partial \zeta_i}{\partial \alpha_t}$$
$$- \sum_i \rho_i \frac{\partial g_i}{\partial \alpha_t} - \sum_i \frac{\partial g_i}{\partial \zeta_i} g_i(\zeta_1, \ldots, \zeta_m, \alpha_i). \quad \text{(A3.4)}$$

Because inequality constraints are employed and because we may assume that the convexity conditions are satisfied, we may invoke the Kuhn–Tucker theorem in examining (A3.4) at the extreme value. This theorem assures us that the quantities in square brackets will either disappear at the extremum or, because we are considering cost minimization, have a positive value. The latter outcome for variable ζ_r can occur only if $\zeta_r = 0$. In this event, the derivative $\frac{\partial \zeta_r}{\partial \alpha_t}$ which appear as the coefficient of the quantity in brackets will have a value of zero. Thus, at an extreme value, the first summation in (A3.4) will disappear.

Using the same theorem and (A3.3a) we note that if a constraint is binding, its value is zero. If it is not, the corresponding Lagrange multiplier is zero. Thus, $\frac{\partial \rho_t}{\partial \alpha_t} = 0$, if the constraint numbered r is not effective. This shows that the last summation in (A3.4) will disappear because either the constraint or its coefficient will be zero.

Now making use of (A3.3b), we have

$$\frac{\partial L^*}{\partial \alpha_t} = \rho_t. \tag{A3.5}$$

Thus, we have shown that when a Lagrangian takes the form of (A3.2), its partial derivative with respect to t equals the corresponding Lagrange multipliers. We will refer to this as the "constraint parameter variation theorem." This is not a new result having been proved as early as 1952 by Cecil Phipps.[2] More recently, Sydney Afriat has considered parametric variations in Lagrangians within a more general context.[3]

A second theorem on parametric variation in a Lagrangian may be obtained by taking the derivative of (A3.2) with respect to β_t. When this is done, we have

$$\frac{\partial L^*}{\partial \beta_t} = \sum_i \left[\frac{\partial f}{\partial \zeta_i} - \sum_i \rho_i \frac{\partial g_i}{\partial \zeta_i} \right] \frac{\partial \zeta_i}{\partial \beta_t} + \frac{\partial f}{\partial \beta_t} - \sum_i \frac{\partial \rho_i}{\partial \beta_t} g_i(\zeta_1, \ldots, \zeta_m, \alpha_i).$$

The same type of reasoning used in the previous theorem will show that each summation is zero at the extreme value. Consequently, at such a value we have

$$\frac{\partial L^*}{\partial \beta_t} = \frac{\partial f}{\partial \beta_t}. \tag{A3.6}$$

For later use, we notice that the $\alpha's$ are constant in this argument. Thus, we have demonstrated that the derivative of a Lagrangian with respect to a parameter in the objective function is equal to the derivative of the objective function with respect to the same parameter. This is referred to as the "objective function parametric valuation theorem."

We now look at the marginal cost of any of the firm's products. We can easily obtain the marginal cost of any of a firm's products by using constant

---

[2]Cecil Glenn Phipps (1952). "The Relation of Differential and Delta Increments," *American Mathematical Monthly*, Vol. 59, pp. 395–398.

[3]Sydney Afriat (1971). "The Theory of Maxima and the Method of Lagrange," *Journal of Applied Mathematics*, Vol. 20, No. 3, pp. 343–357.

parametric variation theory and applying it to (A3.1). We have noticed that x_i in (A3.1) plays the same role as, in (A3.2), when the theorem is applied to (A3.1). Consequently, the last two summations in (A3.1) disappear. As a result, we may show the marginal cost of x_i as

$$\frac{\partial L}{\partial \gamma_t} = \frac{\partial c}{\partial \gamma_t} = \lambda_t. \tag{A3.7}$$

Here, c represents total cost.

We may say now that (A3.7) shows the cost of a small increase in the output of x_t, the other x's remain fixed. But it is difficult to visualize such a change of output. The basic reason is that the change in the factor price parameters would affect more than one product, including perhaps often all products. As a result, the meaning of marginal cost is not operational. We may notice that the definition of marginal cost in (A3.7) plays the same role as α_t in (A3.2). As a consequence of the constraint parameter theorem

$$\frac{\partial L}{\partial z_t} = \frac{\partial c}{\partial z_t} = \mu_t, \tag{A3.8}$$

μ_t is the marginal cost of varying the total quantity of fixed factor t.

To examine the effect of changes of factor prices, we make use of the objective function parameter variation theorem. To do this, we notice that the w's in the Lagrangian (A3.1) are the same as the x's in (A3.2). As before, the x's in (A3.1) correspond to the α's in A3.2.

The objective function parameter variation theorem enables us to apply (A3.6) directly to (A3.1) and further to write

$$\frac{\partial L}{\partial w_t} = \frac{\partial c}{\partial w_l} = \sum_i y_i g_{it}. \tag{A3.9}$$

Equation (A3.9) shows the effect on total cost of a small increase in the price of factor k. It should also be noted that (A3.9) is an extension to the multi-product firm of a result obtained for the single product firm by Samuelson.[4] It should be noted that Samuelson's work pointed to and lead to additional cases. Samuelson is the original and basic pioneer.

---

[4]Paul Samuelson (1947). *Foundations of Economic Analysis*, Cambridge, MA: Harvard University Press.

We will now look at the effect of changes in factor prices. In doing this, we retain the assumption that factor prices are fixed and add the assumption that product prices are fixed by forces external to the firm.

Since the Lagrangian involves the profit function, it can be shown as

$$\hat{L} = \sum_i p_i x_i - \sum_{i=1}^{n} \sum_{j=1}^{m} w_j \, y_{ij} - K(Z_{n1}, \ldots, Z_{ms}) - F - \sum_i w_i z_i - Z_k.$$

(A3.10)

This equation, the firm's profits as the function that should be maximized subject to the constraints on the availability of fixed factors of production.

We notice that the numerical value of the Lagrangian is equal to that of profit because either the constraint or its accompanying Lagrange multiplier will be zero in each case.

To examine the effects of a variation in the price of factor t, we apply the objective function parametric variation theorem to (A3.10) which justifies writing

$$\frac{\partial \hat{L}}{\partial w_t} = \frac{\partial c}{\partial w_l} = -\sum_i y_{it}.$$

(A3.11)

A comparison of (A3.11) with (A3.9) shows that the effect of a factor price increase on profit is the negative of its effect on cost.

We can also use the objective function parameter theorem to find the effect of a product price change on profits. Applying the theorem to (A3.10), we obtain

$$\frac{\partial \hat{L}}{\partial p_k} = \frac{\partial \pi}{\partial p_k} = x_k.$$

(A3.12)

Here, π represents profit. This result is the same as that for a single product firm.

To examine the case of non-parametric factor prices, it is necessary that supply equations for factors be postulated. These are shown as

$$w_j = s_j(y_j, \ldots, y_{nj}, \gamma_j)$$

$$j = 1, \ldots, m.$$

(A3.13)

Clearly, (A3.13) shows that factor prices are influenced by the amount of the factors used by the firm. In addition, the parameters r_s show the effects of influences external to the firm. For example, they could represent the effects of purchases of the factors by other firms which also use the factors in production.

We may substitute (A3.13) into (A3.10), thus obtaining

$$\mathcal{L} = \sum_i p_i x_i - \sum_{i=1}^{n} \sum_{j=1}^{m} s_j y_{ij}(y_{ij}, \ldots, y_{nj}, \gamma) - K(Z_{n1}, \ldots, Z_{ms}) - F$$

$$- \sum_n \gamma_n \left(\sum_i z_{in} - Z_n \right). \tag{A3.14}$$

If the objective function parameters variation theorem is applied to (A3.14), we obtain

$$\frac{\partial \hat{L}}{\partial \gamma_t} = \frac{\partial \pi}{\partial \gamma_t} = - \sum_i y_{it} \left(\frac{\partial \pi}{\partial \gamma_i} \right). \tag{A3.15}$$

Equation (A3.15) may be compared to (A3.11). Clearly, (A3.15) shows the effect of external influences on factor prices explicitly, while (A3.11) may be viewed as a special case of (A3.15).

The consequences of non-parametric product price changes may be investigated by introducing demand equations for the products. These are shown as

$$p_i = g_i(x_i, \ldots, x_n, \varepsilon_i)$$

$$i = 1, \ldots, n. \tag{A3.16}$$

These equations show that quantities produced as variables affect the prices of the products. External influences are represented by the t parameters. These might represent the effects of competitor's actions on the firm's prices for example.

If (A3.16) is substituted into (A3.10), we have

$$\mathcal{L} = x_i g_i(x_1, \ldots, x_m, \epsilon_t) - \sum_{i=1}^{n} \sum_{j=1}^{m} w_j y_{ij} - K(Z_{n1}, \ldots, Z_{ms}). \tag{A3.17}$$

Using the objective function parameter variation theorem in connection with (A3.17) gives

$$\frac{\partial \mathcal{L}}{\partial \epsilon_t} = \frac{\partial \pi}{\partial \epsilon_t} = x_t \left(\frac{\partial p_t}{\partial \epsilon_t} \right). \tag{A3.18}$$

Equation (A3.18) may be compared to (A3.12). It is evident that (A3.12) is a special case of (A3.18). Also, (A3.18) shows that external influences effecting product prices may influence profit.[5]

---

[5]The mathematical evidence in this chapter comes from Ralph W. Pfouts (1973). "Some Cost and Profit Relationship in the Multi-Product Firm," *Southern Economic Journal*, Vol. 39, pp. 351–355.

Appendix 4

Realist Profit and Revenue Seeking: Multi-firm Interaction Effects

Up to this point, we have assumed that, with the firms in their attractors, if $dp_i < 0$, then $dR_i > 0$ and if $dp_i > 0$, then $d\pi_i > 0$. We have put aside the possibility that price changes by competitors might overwhelm i's revenue or profit. We will now obtain the conditions that assure that $dp_i < 0$ implies $dR_i > 0$ and then $dp_i > 0$ means that $d\pi_i > 0$. It will be argued that these conditions will often prevail.

The Revenue Interactions of Price Changes

We will examine the effects of price changes on revenue first and then on profit. To begin this, we write the interfirm effects of price change on revenue in matrix form,

$$
\begin{bmatrix}
0 & p_1 \dfrac{\partial x_1}{\partial p_2} dp_2 & \cdots & p_1 \dfrac{\partial x_1}{\partial p_1} dp_n \\
p_2 \dfrac{\partial x_2}{\partial p_1} dp_1 & 0 & \cdots & p_2 \dfrac{\partial x_{21}}{\partial p_1} dp_n \\
\vdots & & & \\
p_n \dfrac{\partial x_n}{\partial p_1} dp_1 & & p_n \dfrac{\partial x_n}{\partial p_{n-1}} dp_{n-1} & 0
\end{bmatrix}. \quad \text{(A4.1)}
$$

The sum of the ith row of (A4.1) is the sum that appears in (5.1), the change of revenue equation of the ith firm. It will be called the "interior revenue interaction effect" of firm i because it shows the effects of other firm's price changes on the revenue of firm i.

The sum of the ith column is called the "exterior revenue interaction effect" of firm i because it shows the effect of firm i's price change on the revenues of its competitors.

To make use of these two kinds of interaction effects, we define a new variable,

$$\zeta_i = p_i \sum_{k \neq i} \frac{\partial x_i}{\partial p_k} dp_k - \sum_{k \neq i} p_k \frac{\partial x_k}{\partial p_i} dp_i, \qquad (A4.2)$$

which, we call the revenue interaction coefficient for firm i. Clearly, it is the result of subtracting the exterior revenue interaction effect from the interaction effect. To show the meaning of this coefficient, suppose that firm i and some or all of its competitors reduce their prices in an attempt to increase their market shares. Then, the interior revenue interaction effect, the first summation in (A4.2) will be negative because the other firms' price reductions will reduce i's revenue. The exterior revenue interaction effect, the second sum in (A4.2) will be negative because it shows the effects of i's price reduction on the other firms' revenues. But the minus sign that precedes it makes the effect positive showing it as a benefit for firm i. Thus, if $\zeta_i > 0$, i has benefitted from the price changes because the second sum is larger in absolute amount than the first, showing that the loss of revenue inflicted by i is greater than the loss of revenue it suffered from other firms' price cuts; i inflicted more damage than it sustained. In other words, if $\zeta_i > 0$, i is a winner in price competition. If $\zeta_i < 0$, the opposite is true and it is a loser in price competition.

Perhaps, it should be stressed that in defining and using ζ_i we are doing something unusual. We are considering not only the effect of competitors' price changes on firm i's revenue as given by the first term on the right side of (A4.2) but also the effect of i's price changes on its competitors' revenues shown by the second term on the right side of (A4.2). Further, we are subtracting the effect of i on competitors' revenue from their effect on i's revenue to get a net effect. We are assuming that a loss of revenue by competitors adds as much to i's competitive position as a gain of revenue by i. In this way, we gain a more complete measure of the results of price competition.

A final point about the coefficient of revenue interaction can be made. If we add the coefficients for all firms we get zero, i.e.,

$$\sum_{i=1}^{n} \zeta_i = \sum_{i=1}^{n} p_i \sum_{k \neq i} \frac{\partial x_i}{\partial p_k} dp_k - \sum_{i=1}^{n} p_i \sum_{k \neq i} p_k \frac{\partial x_k}{\partial p_i} dp_i = 0. \qquad (A4.3)$$

This must be true because the first summation on the right totals all the elements in (A4.1) by rows while the second sum on the right adds all the elements by columns. Thus, if $\zeta_i > 0$, there must be at least one firm with a negative coefficient. There must be winners and losers in price competition. This is true even if only one firm changes its price.

To deal further with price interaction, we define an additional variable

$$E_i = x_i dp_i + p_i \frac{\partial x_i}{\partial p_i} dp_i + \sum_{k \neq i} p_k \frac{\partial x_k}{\partial p_k} dp_i > 0, \qquad (A4.4)$$

where $dp_i < 0$ and the firm is in its attractor. E_i shows the effect of firm i's price cut on revenues of all the firms. The own price effect, the first two terms on the right, will be positive if the firm's demand is elastic as it would be in an attractor. The summation shows the effect of the price change on competing firms, and, in this case where $dp_i < 0$, will be negative and smaller in absolute amount than i's own price effect.

This can be restated by saying that the effect of firm i's price cut is stronger on the sales of its own product than on the sales of its competitors. This outcome has sometimes been assumed in both theoretical and applied economic analysis. To convince oneself that it is true, one may assume that it is not true and consider the results.

If (A4.4) is not true, then the firm affects other firms' sales more strongly than it affects its own. Thus, it might have trouble increasing or decreasing its sales but could more readily affect the sales of competitors. To affect its own sales, it might have to arrange for another firm to change its price, or perhaps, for a number of other firms to do so. In turn, it might be solicited by competitors who want it to change its price to accommodate their sales. Thus, a competitor might ask a firm to raise its price to improve sales for the competitor which in turn would offer to raise its price to help the sales of the firm that was approached. Contradictory situation arise immediately.

A more formal reduction *ad absurdum* can be put forward. If (A4.4) is not true, then it must be true that

$$E_i = x_i dp_i + p_i \frac{\partial x_i}{\partial p_i} dp_i + \sum_{k \neq i} p_k \frac{\partial x_k}{\partial p_k} dp_i \leq 0.$$

If we move the summation to the right-hand side and add the interior revenue interaction effect to each side, we obtain

$$x_i dp_i + p_i \frac{\partial x_i}{\partial p_i} dp_i + p_i \sum_{k \neq i} p_k \frac{\partial x_k}{\partial p_k} dp_k$$

$$\leq p_i \sum_{k \neq i} p_k \frac{\partial x_k}{\partial p_k} dp_k - \sum_{k \neq i} p_k \frac{\partial x_k}{\partial p_k} dp_i, \qquad (A4.5)$$

or

$$dR_i \leq \zeta_i.$$

The last relation is very unlikely to occur because economic intuition would suggest rather strongly that the firm's change in revenue would be greater than its net change in revenue interaction. In addition, (A4.5) says that the change in revenue can never be greater than the net revenue interaction effect. Further, it says that if the firm is a loser in price competition, if $\zeta_i < 0$, then it has undergone a loss of revenue. The own price effect cannot overcome the competitive loss. This not only violates economic intuition but it also outrages common sense.

An additional point can be made. Suppose that all the firms lowered their prices. Then, (A4.5) becomes

$$\sum_{j=1}^{n} dR_i \zeta_i = \sum_{i=1}^{n} \zeta_i = 0.$$

This says that, even though all firms lower their price, the change of total revenue is never positive.

These absurd results hold if and only if (A4.4) does not hold. Consequently, we accept (A4.4).

We are now in a position to take up the question of how dR_i will be positive unless the interior interaction effect is negative and larger in absolute amount than the own price effect. But merely saying this does little to relate this outcome to other variables in the model.

To examine the question in a different way, we note that (A4.1), (A4.4), and (A4.2) enable us to write

$$dR_i - E_i = \zeta_i,$$

where $dp_i < 0$ and $E_i > 0$. We rewrite this as

$$dR_i = E_i + \zeta_i > 0, \qquad (A4.6)$$

which is the desired result.

If $\zeta_i > 0$, if the firm is a winner in the price competition, then (A4.6) holds. If $\zeta_i < 0$, if the firm is a loser in the price competition, then (A4.6) will hold if and only if $E_i > -\zeta_i$. E_i must be larger than the absolute amount of ζ_i. This is clearly possible even though the firm loses in price competition.

E_i is the entire effect of firm i's price decrease while ζ_i is the difference between i's interior price effect and its exterior price effect. Economic intuition would suggest that E_i would usually be larger.

The importance of the relative size of the price decrease is evident. If dp_i is large in absolute amount, this increases the positive part of ζ_i, the right most summation, thus improving i's effect in price competition. A large value of price change also increases the own price effect in E_i, which contributes to making dR_i positive. These points may be verified by examining (A4.2) and (A4.4).

The Profits Interactions of Price Changes

To analyze the interfirm effects of price changes on profits we, using (A4.3), arrange them in matrix form. We are assuming that the firms are in their attractors and that $dp_j > 0$ for all firms.

$$
\begin{bmatrix}
0 & \left(p_1 - \dfrac{\partial k_1}{\partial x_1}\right)\dfrac{\partial x_1}{\partial p_2}dp_2 \\[2mm]
\left(p_2 - \dfrac{\partial k_2}{\partial x_1}\right)\dfrac{\partial x_2}{\partial p_1}dp_1 & 0 \\[2mm]
\vdots & \\[2mm]
\left(p_n - \dfrac{\partial k_n}{\partial x_n}\right)\dfrac{\partial x_n}{\partial p_1}dp_1 & \cdots \\[4mm]
& \cdots \quad \left(p_1 - \dfrac{\partial k_1}{\partial x_1}\right)\dfrac{\partial x_1}{\partial p_n}dp_n \\[2mm]
& \left(p_2 - \dfrac{\partial k_2}{\partial x_2}\right)\dfrac{\partial x_2}{\partial p_n}dp_n \\[2mm]
& \vdots \\[2mm]
\left(p_n - \dfrac{\partial k_n}{\partial x_n}\right)\dfrac{\partial x_n}{\partial p_{n-1}}dp_{n-1} & 0
\end{bmatrix}. \quad (A4.7)
$$

The sum of row j is the interior profit interaction effect for firm j. The sum of column j is the exterior profit interaction effect for firm j. These definitions clearly parallel those for revenue.

Similarly, we define

$$
\xi_i = \sum_{k \neq i}\left(p_i - \frac{\partial x_k}{\partial x_i}\right)\frac{\partial x_i}{\partial p_k}dp_k - \sum_{k \neq i}\left(p_k - \frac{\partial x_k}{\partial p_k}\right)\frac{\partial x_k}{\partial p_i}dp_i, \quad (A4.8)
$$

ξ_i is the profit interaction coefficient. The right side of (A4.8) is arranged so that when i benefits from the price interactions, ξ_i will be positive. If it is negative, firm i has lost in the price interactions. These results follow because the first summation in (A4.8) shows the effect on firm i's profit of competitors raising their prices. Their price increases expand the demand for i's product, and segments profit, thus showing a negative effect. A price increase has the same effect on the profits of competitors but the minus sign makes the effect on ξ_i positive i has done more damage to its competitors profits than its competitors have done to i's profit. In this sense, i is a winner if $\xi_i > 0$. Of course, the opposite outcome results in $\xi_i < 0$.

As we did with revenue, we use the loss or gain of profit by competitors as a consequence of i's actions, as being as important to i's competitive position as its own gain or loss of profit. Our definition of ξ_i in (A4.8) shows this.

We also notice that, as was the case with the revenue interaction coefficients, the total of the profit interaction coefficients is zero.

$$\sum_{i=1}^{n} \xi_i = \sum_{i=1}^{n} \sum_{k \neq i} \left(p_k - \frac{\partial x_k}{\partial x_k} \right) \frac{\partial x_k}{\partial p_i} dp_k$$

$$- \sum_{i=1}^{n} \sum_{k \neq i} \left(p_k - \frac{\partial x_k}{\partial p_k} \right) \frac{\partial x_k}{\partial p_i} dp_i = 0. \qquad (A4.9)$$

As we did with revenue, we will rely on an expression that shows all of the effects on the profits of all the firms of a price increase by firm i,

$$\bar{E}_i = x_i dp_i + \left(p_i - \frac{\partial k_i}{\partial x_i} \right) \frac{\partial x_i}{\partial p_i} dp_i + \sum_{k \neq i} \left(p_k - \frac{\partial k_k}{\partial x_k} \right) \frac{\partial x_k}{\partial p_i} dp_i > 0.$$

$$(A4.10)$$

We believe $\bar{E}_i$ to be positive because it shows the consequences for the profits of all firms of a price increase by firm i with the firms inside their attractors also if it is negative or zero it leads to strange results.

To demonstrate this we note that if $\bar{E}_i$ is not positive than (A4.10) is not true so that

$$\bar{E}_i = x_i dp_i + \left(p_i - \frac{\partial k_i}{\partial x_i} \right) \frac{\partial x_i}{\partial p_i} dp_i + \sum_{k \neq i} \left(p_k - \frac{\partial k_k}{\partial x_k} \right) \frac{\partial x_k}{\partial p_i} dp_i \leq 0.$$

We now move the summation to the right side and add the interior profit interaction effect to each side obtaining

$$x_i dp_i + \left(p_i - \frac{\partial k_i}{\partial x_i} \right) \frac{\partial x_i}{\partial p_i} dp_i + \sum_{k \neq i} \left(p_k - \frac{\partial k_k}{\partial x_k} \right) \frac{\partial x_k}{\partial p_i} dp_i$$

$$\leq \sum_{k \neq 1} \left(p_i - \frac{\partial k_i}{\partial x_i} \right) \frac{\partial x_i}{\partial p_k} dp_k - \sum_{k \neq i} \left(p_k - \frac{\partial k_k}{\partial x_k} \right) \frac{\partial x_k}{\partial p_i} dp_i,$$

or

$$dπ_i \leq ξ_i. \tag{A4.11}$$

This is unlikely to be true because it says that no firm can increase its profit by raising its price when $ξ_i < 0$, when it loses in profit competition price changes. Own price effect is always less than the competitive effect. This is unrealistic.

If all firms are in their attractors and each raises its price we have

$$\sum_{k \neq i} dπ_i \leq \sum_{i=1}^{n} ξ_i = 0.$$

The total change of profit when all firms are in their attractors and all raise prices cannot be positive. This result coupled with (A4.11) cause us to assume that (A4.10) holds.

We now take up the question of when $dp_i > 0$ implies that $dπ_i > 0$.

Clearly, (A4.3), (A4.8), and (A4.10) enable us to write

$$dπ_i = \bar{E}_i + ξ_i,$$

while keeping in mind that $dp_i > 0$, $\bar{E}_i > 0$ and the firm is in its attractor. We rewrite the preceding as

$$dπ_i = \bar{E}_i + ξ_i > 0. \tag{A4.12}$$

If the firm was a winner in price competition, if $ξ_i > 0$, then clearly (A4.12) holds. If the firm was a loser in price competition, if $ξ_i < 0$, then (A4.12) holds if and only if $\bar{E}_i = -ξ_i$. $\bar{E}_i$ must be larger than the absolute amount of $ξ_i$.

$\bar{E}_i$ being the entire profit effect of i's price increase would often be expected to be larger in absolute amount than $ξ_i$, the difference between internal and external profit effects of price changes. But it clearly is possible for $ξ_i$ to be larger in absolute amount though it might happen infrequently.

The relative size of the price changes is important for profit just as it was for revenue. A small price change by firm i means a small value for the second term on the right of (A4.8), thus providing only a small offset to first term on the right and consequently a large absolute value of $ξ_i$. A small price increase by i also means that own price effect on profit will be small which means a small value for $\bar{E}_i$.

Appendix 5

Realist Retail Satisficing

During the latter part of the 19th century, through the 20th century and well into the 21st century the standard of living in the United States increased greatly. This reflects increasing production and distribution of goods and services.

We have already given attention to the production of goods and services, but we have not yet looked at the distribution of goods and services. We can notice easily that most goods and many services are distributed by large — actually huge — stores.[1] Further, we can observe that a company may consist of a number, perhaps a large number of giant stores. These stores are part of large companies each of which usually covers a considerable geographical portion of the United States.

How does it operate? If the company is very large, if it includes a large number of giant stores, it will usually operate in a large number of cities. Thus, it will spread over a large section of the country. The large section is divided into a few, somewhat smaller sections. Each section has a headquarters.

Thus, a large company might have its headquarters in Los Angeles with regional headquarters in San Diego, Seattle, Phoenix, Denver, and Boise. All the stores operating in the Northwest would report to the office in Seattle. Other cities would also be centers for stores in their areas.

---

[1] Ralph W. Pfouts (1997). "Profit Maximization in Chain Retail Stores," *Journal of Industrial Economics*, Vol. 27, pp. 69–83.

There are two basic questions that must be considered to provide a basic organization for the entire business. The first is who establishes prices and how is it done? The second question is who determines what will be included in the stores. In other words what goods and services will be offered by the stores?

The answers to these questions distribute authority within part of the company in each area.

The first question's answer usually is that the prices are established at the regional headquarters. Thus, a store in Colorado Springs would have prices established in Denver, not in Colorado Springs or Los Angeles.

The second question is who decides what is included in the stores. The manager of the store in Colorado Springs would decide what should be available in the store.

This brief description indicates that while ultimate authority resides in the national headquarters, Los Angeles in the example, regional headquarters, Denver and the store itself also have some authority.

Another important question is how are pricing decisions made? Presumably they are made in regional headquarters, Denver in our example. But decisions in regional headquarters are subject to some external influences, as will be seen.

Selling a good depends on the quality of the good, its price and location in the store. The quality of the good depends on its design and manufacture. The price of the good depends on the selling company's executives in the regional headquarters.

Selling the good also depends to an appreciable and recognized extent on its location in the store. The "shelf space", as the location of goods within the store is called, is important in bringing the good to the attention of customers and in adding or detracting to or from the appearance of the good. A store will have refrigerated space, freezer space, regular shelf space, specially designed shelf space and end of counter space, etc.

Thus, in selling merchandise, both its price and presentation are important. Price is established and controlled at the regional headquarters, Denver in our example.

A method of establishing price is to use a specified markup on the price paid by the store for a particular good. The objection made to this is that it does not pay attention to the demand for the product. This is not an accurate statement. The price paid for a product is a market price and consequentially depends on the demand for the product. The addition of a markup by the store is certainly going to reflect demand in the market in which the product was purchased; that is, the cost of the item is increased (marked up) by a certain percentage. The outcome is the sale price of the item.

Also, a Langrangian method of pricing and selling products could be used. But a serious problem in doing this is that usually all the required data and information will not be completely available. Some of the data could be faked and a conclusion reached, but the faked information lessens the dependability of the Lagrangian method.

A perhaps better method is to study the sources of profit in the past and plan the emphasis of sales of goods to be varied with heavy emphasis on the goods that have been rich sources of profit in the past.

The development of food stores led to developments in retailing in other fields. For example large chain drugstores have developed. They are in many respects similar to giant grocery stores.

Like the grocery chains much of their merchandise is perishable. As a result the policies within drugstore chains tend to be much the same as within the huge food companies. But most drugs probably have longer shelf lives.

An interview with a former executive in a large drug chain revealed that the organization of the drug chain duplicated the huge food chains, but he thought there were fewer spoilage problems among the drugs than there were among foods.

No doubt he represented the drug chain for which he had worked very accurately. He believed also that most of the existing drug chains were similar to food store chains.

Let us provisionally accept the former drug chain executive's assessment that the food chains and the drug chains are quite similar. After all they both deal to a considerable extent with goods that have short existences, so they will not hold a high percentage of their inventories in goods that may spoil. Are department stores likely to emulate their behavior? One might suppose that they would handle their inventory policy differently. However, all three act very similarly. Why?

There clearly is more than one reason why department stores are becoming chain stores, why they follow the practices of existing chain stores.

No doubt there are a number of reasons for the development of chain stores among department stores. First, it puts your company to work in huge markets. You can extend your market from city to city. This enlarges your growth potential and encourages your staff and your owners (shareholders). Your firm has great growth potential. Growth potential is usually a very strong growth stimulant.

There is another reason why many kinds of business and many kinds of firms may follow giant grocery stores, drugstores, and department stores. In each case there have been successful stores and thus, successful firms.

To what further stages of development will this lead us? Who can say? We can logically have limited conclusions or we might have a very limited knowledge of the future. Joseph Schumpeter understood that development was a major part of what was happening and what people were doing.[2] He also understood that economies change and developed. Capitalism is an evolutionary realist process more than a simple neoclassical idealist exercise.[3]

---

[2]Joseph Schumpeter (1942, 1947). *Capitalism Socialism and Democracy*, 2nd ed., New York and London: Harper and Brothers, p. 82.

[3]Ross Tucker (2013). "How 'Big Grocery' is Starting to Bite Consumers," Available at http://finance.yahoo.com/blogs/the-exchange/how–big-grocery–is-starting-to-bite-consumers-174111863.html.

Bibliography

Afriat, Sydney (1971). "The Theory of Maxima and the Method of Lagrange," *Journal of Applied Mathematics*, Vol. 20, No. 3, pp. 343–357.

Allen, Reginald (2006). *Plato: The Republic*, New Haven: Yale University Press.

Anderson, Perry (1974). *Lineages of the Absolutist State*, London: Verso.

Aoki, Masahiko (2001). *Information, Incentives and Bargaining in the Japanese Economy*, Oxford: Oxford University Press.

Arens, Edmund and Smith, David (1994). *The Logic of Pragmatic Thinking: From Peirce to Habermas*, New York: Prometheus Books.

Ariel Rubinstein (1998). *Modeling Bounded Rationality*, MIT Press.

Arrow, Kenneth (1950). "A Difficulty in the Concept of Social Welfare," *Journal of Political Economy*, Vol. 58, No. 4, August, pp. 328–346.

Arrow, Kenneth (1963). *Social Choice and Individual Values*, 2nd edn, New York: Wiley.

Arrow, Kenneth J. (1987). "Rationality of self and others in an economic system," in R. M. Hogarth and M. W. Reder (eds.), *Rational Choice*, Chicago: The University of Chicago Press.

Aslund, Anders (1995). *Building Capitalism: The Transformation of the Former Soviet Bloc*, Cambridge: Cambridge University Press.

Aslund, Anders (2001). *How Russia Became a Market Economy*, Washington DC: Brookings.

Aslund, Anders (2007). *Russia's Capitalist Revolution: Why Market Reform Succeeded and Democracy Failed*, Washington DC: Peterson Institute.

Bailey, M. J. (1954). "Price and Output Determination by a Firm Selling Retailed Products," *American Economic Review*, Vol. 44, pp. 82–95.

Baldwin, Richard and Wyplosz, Charles (2012). *The Economics of European Integration*, 4th edn, New York: McGraw Hill.

Barro, Robert (1989). "The Ricardian Approach to Budget Deficits," *The Journal of Economic Perspectives*, Vol. 3, No. 2. http://www.ukzn.ac.za/economics/viegi/teaching/uct/barro.pdf.

Bate, Robert (2009). "What Is Prosperity and How Do We Measure It?" *AEI online*, Tuesday, October 27, 2009.

Baumol, William (1959). *Business Behavior, Value and Growth* (rev. ed), New York: Macmillan.

Beltrami, Edward (1987). *Mathematics for Dynamic Modeling*, Boston: Academic Press.

Benjamin, Ward (1958). "The Firm in Illyria: Market Syndicalism," *American Economic Review*, Vol. 48, No. 4, pp. 566–589.

Bentham, Jeremy (1776). *A Fragment on Government*, London.

Bergson, Abram (1938). "A Reformulation of Certain Aspects of Welfare Economics," *Quarterly Journal of Economics*, Vol. 52, No. 1, pp. 310–334.

Bergson, Abram (1954). "The Concept of Social Welfare," *Quarterly Journal of Economics*, Vol. 68, No. 2, pp. 233–253.

Bergson, Abram (1966). "Socialist Calculation," in Bergson (ed.), *Essays in Normative Economics*, Cambridge, MA: Harvard University Press.

Bergson, Abram (1976). "Social Choice and Welfare Economics Under Representative Government," *Journal of Economics*, Vol. 6, No. 3 (October), pp. 171–190.

Bergson, Abram (1978). *Productivity and the Social System — The USSR and the West*, Harvard University Press, Cambridge, MA.

Bergson, Abram (1991). "The USSR Before the Fall: How Poor and Why?" *Journal of Economic Perspectives*, No. 5, Fall, pp. 29–44.

Bergson, Abram (1938). "A Reformulation of Certain Aspects of Welfare Economics," *Quarterly Journal of Economics*, Vol. 52, No. 1, pp. 210–234.

Bergstrom, Theodore. "*The Rotten Kid Theorem*," The New Palgrave Dictionary of Economics, London: Palgrave Macmillan, 2008. http://www.dictionaryofeconomics.com/dictionary.

Berle, Adolf and Means, Gardner (1932). *The Modern Corporation and Private Property*, New York: Macmillan.

Berliner, Joseph (1978). *The Innovation Decision in Soviet Industry*, Cambridge MA: MIT Press.

Birman, Igor (1983). *Экономика недостач*. Нью-Йорк: Chalidze publications.

Buchanan, James (1999). *Democracy in Deficit: The Political Legacy of Lord Keynes*, Indianapolis, IN: Liberty Fund.

Buchanan, James and Tollison, Robert (1975). *The Limits of Liberty Between Anarchy and Leviathan*, Chicago: University of Chicago Press.

Burke, Peter J. and Jan E. Stets (2009). *Identity Theory*. New York: Oxford University Press.

Buss, David (2008). *Evolutionary Psychology: The New Science of the Mind*, Boston: Omegatype.

Chen, Yun and Ken Morita (2012). "Toward an East Asian Community," in Steven Rosefielde, Masaaki Kuboniwa and Satoshi Mizobata (eds.), *Prevention and Crisis Management: Lessons for Asia from the 2008 Crisis*, Singapore: World Scientific 2012.

Chiasson, Phyllis (2001). *Peirce's Pragmatism: The Design for Thinking*, Amsterdam: Rodopi.

Clemens, E. W. (1951). "Price Discrimination and its Multi-Product Firm," *Review of Economic Studies*, Vol. 19, pp. 1–11.

Cole, George Douglas Howard (1917). *Guild Socialism Re-Stated*, London: L. Parsons.

Cole, George Douglas Howard (1920). *Self-Government in Industry*, London: G. Bell.

Conn, David (1979). "A Comparison of Alternative Incentive Structures for Centrally Planned Economic Systems," *Journal of Comparative Economics*, Vol. 3, No. 3, pp. 235–253.

D'Aveni, Richard (1994). *Hypercompetition: Managing the Dynamics of Strategic Maneuvering*, New York: Free Press.

Dahl, Robert (1971). *Polyarchy: Participation and Opposition*, New Haven: Yale University Press.

Denton, Derek (2006). *The Primordial Emotions: The Dawning of Consciousness*, London: Oxford University Press.

Derrida, Jacques (1973). *Speech and Phenomena and Other Essays on Husserl's Theory of Signs*, Evanston: Northwestern University Press.

Descartes, Rene (1641). *Meditations on First Philosophy*.

Domar, Evsei (1966), "The Soviet Collective Farm as a Producer Cooperative," *American Economic Review*, Vol. 56, No. 4, pp. 734–757.

Dorfman, Robert (1951). *Application of Linear Programming to the Theory of the Firm*, Berkeley: University of California Press.

Dorfman, Robert (1958). Samuelson, Paul and Robert Solow, *Linear Programming and Economic Analysis*, New York: McGraw-Hill.

Dreyfus, Hubert (1990). *Being-in-the-World: A Commentary on Heidegger's Being and Time, Division I*, Cambridge MA: MIT Press.

Dunlop, John and Fedorenko, Nikolay (1969). *Planning and Markets: Modern Trends in Various Economic Systems*, New York: McGraw Hill.

Ellman, Michael (1971). *Soviet Planning Today, Proposals for an Optimally Functioning Economic System*, Cambridge: Cambridge University Press.

Ericson, Richard (2006). "Command Versus 'Shadow': The Conflicted Soul of the Soviet Economy," *Comparative Economic Studies*, Vol. 48, No. 1, pp. 50–76.

Fedorenko, Nikolay (1974). *Optimal Functioning System for a Socialist Economy*, Moscow: Progress, Moscow.

Festinger, Leon (1957). *A Theory of Cognitive Dissonance*, Stanford, CA: Stanford University Press.

Fisher, Irving (1974). *The Theory of Interest*, Clifton New Jersey: Augustus M. Kelley (originally published in 1930).

Fox, Elaine (2008). *Emotion Science: An Integration of Cognitive and Neuroscientific Approaches*, New York: Palgrave MacMillan.

Freud, Sigmund (1922). *Beyond the Pleasure Principle*.

Freud, Sigmund (1923). *The Ego and the Id (Das Ich und das Es)*.

Freud, Sigmund (1930). *Civilization and its Discontents* [*Das Unbehagen in der Kultur* ("The Uneasiness in Culture")].

Fromm, Erich (1967). *Socialist Humanism*, London: Allen Lane/Penguin Press.

Fromm, Erich (1992). *The Revision of Psychoanalysis*, Colorado: Westview Press.

Fromm, Erich, Suzuki, D. T. and Martino, Richard De (1960). *Zen Buddhism and Psychoanalysis*, New York: Harper Colophon Books.

Gadamer, Hans-Georg (2004). *Truth and Method*, 2nd rev. edn. Trans. J. Weinsheimer and D. G. Marshall, New York: Crossroad.

Gerschenkron, Alexander (1962). "Russia: Patterns and Problems of Economic Development, 1861–1958," in Gerschenkron (ed.), *Economic Backwardness in Historical Perspective*, Cambridge, MA: Harvard University Press, pp. 119–151.

Gigerenzer, Gerd and Selten, Reinhard (2002). *Bounded Rationality: The Adaptive Toolbox*. Cambridge: MIT Press.

Gini, Corrado (1921). "Measurement of the Inequality of Incomes," *The Economic Journal*, Vol. 31, 1921, pp. 124–126.

Goodfriend, Marvin (2011). "Central Banking in the Credit Turmoil: An Assessment of Federal Reserve Practice," *Journal of Monetary Economics*, Vol. 58, pp. 1–12.

Grauwe, Paul De (2000). *Economics of Monetary Union*, New York: Oxford University Press.

Grauwe, Paul De (2010). "Top-Down versus Bottom-Up Macroeconomics," *CESifo Economic Studies*, Vol. 56, No. 4, pp. 465–497.

Grossman, G. (1963). "Notes for a Theory of the Command Economy," *Soviet Studies*, Vol. 15, No. 2, 1963, pp. 101–123.

Gross, John (2008). *The Theory of Adaptive Economic Behavior*, Cambridge: Cambridge University Press.

Grossman, Gregory (1977). "The 'Second Economy' of the USSR," *Problems of Communism*, Vol. 26, No. 5, 1977, pp. 25–40.

Greenberg, Joseph (1979). "Existence and Optimality of Equilibrium in Labor-Managed Economies," *Review of Economic Studies*, Vol. 46, pp. 419–433.

Habermas, Jurgen (1954). *Moral Consciousness and Communicative Action*, MIT Press: Cambridge, MA, 1990.

Habermas, Jurgen (1984). *Theory of Communicative Action Volume One: Reason and the Rationalization of Society*, Beacon Press: Boston.

Haidt, Jonathan (2006). *The Happiness Hypothesis: Find Modern Truth in Ancient Wisdom*, New York: Basic Books.

Haidt, Jonathan (2013). *The Righteous Mind: Why Good People Are Divided by Politics and Religion*, New York: Vintage.

Harsanyi, John and Selten, Richard (1988). *A General Theory of Equilibrium Selection in Games*, Cambridge: MIT Press.

Hegel, Georg Wilhelm Friedrich (2004). *Phenomenology of Spirit*, London: Oxford University Press.

Heidegger, Martin (1977). *Sein und Zeit*, in Heidegger's Gesamtausgabe, Volume 2, ed. F.-W. von Herrmann, XIV.

Hothersall, David (2003). *History of Psychology*, New York: McGraw-Hill.

Jehle, Geoffrey and Reny, Philip (1998). *Advanced Microeconomic Theory*, Boston: Addison Wesley.

Jevons, William Stanley (1863). *A General Mathematical Theory of Political Economy*.

Jevons, William Stanley (1871). *The Theory of Political Economy*.

Jung, Carl (1972). *Two Essays on Analytical Psychology*, Princeton NJ: Princeton University Press.

Kahn, Richard (1931). "The Relation of Home Investment to Unemployment," *Economic Journal*, Vol. 41, No. 162, pp. 173–198.

Kahneman, Daniel (2003). "Maps of Bounded Rationality: Psychology for Behavioral Economics," *The American Economic Review*, Vol. 93, No. 5, pp. 1449–1475.

Kaiser, Wolfram and Starie, Peter (eds.) (2009). *Transnational European Union: Towards a Common Political Space*, London: Routledge.

Kant, Immanuel (2005). *Groundwork of the Metaphysic of Morals*, New York: Harper and Row Publishers.

Kant, Immanuel (2011). *The Critique of Pure Reason*, New York: CreateSpace Independent Publishing Platform.

Kenen, Peter B. (1967). "Toward a Supranational Monetary System," in G. Pontecorvo, R. P. Shay, and A. G. Hart (eds.), *Issues in Banking and Monetary Analysis*, New York: Holt, Reinhart, and Winston.

Keynes, John Maynard (1920). *The Economic Consequences of the Peace*, New York: Harcourt Brace.

Keynes, John Maynard (1936). *The General Theory of Employment, Interest and Money*, London: Macmillan Cambridge University Press, for Royal Economic Society.

Kihlstron, Richard and Laffont, Jean-Jacques (2002). "General Equilibrium in a Labor-Managed Economy with Uncertainty and Incomplete Markets," *Annals of Economics and Finance*, Vol. 3, pp. 185–217.

Kimmenl, Michael (1988). *Absolutism and Its Discontents: State and Society in Seventeenth-Century France and England*, New Brunswick, NJ: Transaction Books.

Krugman, Paul (2009). *The Return of Depression Economics and the Crisis of 2008*, New York: W.W. Norton Company, 2009.

Kuhn, Thomas (1962). *The Structure of Scientific Revolutions*, Chicago: University of Chicago Press.

Kydland, Phillip and Prescott, Edward (1982). "Time to Build and Aggregate Fluctuations," *Econometrica*, Vol. 50, No. 6, pp. 1345–1370.

Laffont, Jean-Jacques and Tirole, Jean (1993). *A Theory of Incentives in Procurement and Regulation*, Cambridge MA: MIT Press.

Laville, F. (2000). "Should We Abandon Optimization Theory? The Need for Bounded Rationality," *The Journal of Economic Methodology*, 7, 2000, pp. 395–426.

Leibniz, Gottfried (1710). *Essais de Theodicee sur la bonte de Dieu, la liberte de l'homme et l'origine du mal.*

Lewis, Tracy and Sappington, David (1993). "Ignorance in Agency Problems," *Journal of Economic Theory*, Vol. 61, pp. 169–183.

Lipset, Seymore (1983). *Political Man: The Social Bases of Politics*, London: Heinemann.

Locke, John (1689). *An Essay Concerning Human Understanding.*

Lucas, Robert Jr. (1972). "Expectations and the Neutrality of Money", *Journal of Economic Theory*, Vol. 4, No. 2, pp. 103–124.

Lucas, Robert Jr. (2003). "Macroeconomic Priorities," *American Economic Review*, Vol. 93, No. 1, pp. 1–14.

Malia, Martin (1994). *The Soviet Tragedy: A History of Socialism in Russia, 1917–1991*, The Free Press.

Mann, Thomas and Norman Ornstein (2013). *It's Even Worse Than It Looks: How the American Constitutional System Collided With the New Politics of Extremism*, New York: Basic Books.

Marglin, Stephen (2008). *The Dismal Science: How Thinking like an Economist Undermines Community*, Cambridge MA: Harvard University Press.

Marvin Goodfriend (2011). "Central Banking in the Credit Turmoil: An Assessment of Federal Reserve Practice," *Journal of Monetary Economics*, Vol. 58, pp. 1–12.

Maskin, Eric and Tirole, Jean (1990). "The Principal–Agent Relationship with an Informed Principal, I: Private Values," *Econometrica*, Vol. 58, pp. 379–410.

Maskin, Eric and Tirole, Jean (1992). "The Principal–Agent Relationship with an Informed Principal, II: Common Values," *Econometrica*, Vol. 60, pp. 1–42.

May, K. O. (1954). "Intransitivity, Utility and the Aggregation of Preference Patterns," *Econometrica*, Vol. 22, pp. 1–13.

McCauley, Joseph (2003). "Thermodynamic Analogies in Economics and Finance: Instability of Markets," *Physica*, Vol. 329, pp. 199–212.

McCloskey, Donald (Deidre) (1993). "Review of Alexander Rosenberg, Mathematic Politics or Science of Diminishing Returns", *The History of Science Society*, Vol. 84, No. 4, pp. 838–839.

McCloskey, Deidre (2007). *The Bourgeois Virtues: Ethics for an Age of Commerce*, Chicago: University of Chicago Press.

McKinnon, Ronald (1963). "Optimum Currency Areas," *American Economic Review*, Vol. 53, No. 4, pp. 717–725.

Meade, James (1993). *Liberty, Equality and Efficiency*, New York: New York University Press.

Mundell, Robert A. (1961). "A Theory of Optimum Currency Areas," *American Economic Review*, Vol. 51, pp. 657–664.

Neuberger, Egon (1966). "Libermanism, Computopia and the Visible Hand: The Question of Informational Efficiency," *American Economic Review*, Vol. 56, No. 1/2, pp. 131–144.

Neumann, John von and Morgenstern, Oskar (2007). *Theory of Games and Economic Behavior (Commenorative Edition)*, Princeton NJ: Princeton University Press.

Nonneman, Walter (2007). *European Immigration and the Labor Market, The Transatlantic Task Force on Immigration and Integration*, Migration Policy Institute, Bertelsmann Stiftung.

Nove, Alec (1977). *The Soviet Economic System*, London: George Allen and Unwin.

Nuti, Domenico Mario (2013). "Euroarea: Premature, Diminished, Divergent," *Social Europe Journal*. http://www.social-europe.eu/2013/08/the-euroarea-premature-diminished-divergent/.

Olson, Robert G. (1967). "Deontological Ethics," in: Paul Edwards (ed.), *The Encyclopedia of Philosophy*, London: Collier Macmillan.

Pareto, Vilfredo (1906). *Manuel of Political Economy*.

Peirce, Charles Sanders (1985). *Historical Perspectives on Peirce's Logic of Science: A History of Science* (2 Volumes), New York: Mouton De Graytes.

Peirce, Charles Sanders (1997). *Pragmatism as a Principle and Method of Right Thinking*, ("Lectures on Pragmatism 1903," edited by Patricia Turisi), Stoneybrook: State University of New York Press.

Peirce, Charles Sanders (2010). *Philosophy of Mathematics: Selected Writings*, Bloomington: Indiana University Press.

Pfouts, Ralph W. (1961). "The Theory of Cost and Production in the Multi-Product Firm," *Econometrica*, Vol. 29, pp. 650–658.

Pfouts, Ralph W. (1964). "Multi-Product Firm vs. Single-Product Firms: The Theory of Cost and Production," *Metroeconomica*, Vol. 16, pp. 51–66.

Pfouts, Ralph W. (1973). "Some Cost and Profit Relationship in the Multi-Product Firm," *Southern Economic Journal*, Vol. 39, pp. 351–355.

Pfouts, Ralph W. (1997). "Profit Maximization in Chai Retail Stores," *Journal of Industrial Economics*, Vol. 27, pp. 69–83.

Phipps, Cecil Glenn (1952). "The Relation of Differential and Delta Increments," *American Mathematical Monthly*, Vol. 59, 1952, pp. 395–398.

Plato (1967). *Plato in Twelve Volumes*, Vol. 3 translated by W. R. M. Lamb, Cambridge, MA, Harvard University Press.

Plato (1994). *Republic*, trans. Robin Waterfield, Oxford: Oxford University Press.

Popper, Karl (1945). *The Open Society and Its Enemies* (2 Volumes), London: Routledge.

Popper, Karl (1963). *Conjectures and Refutations: The Growth of Scientific Knowledge*, London: Routledge.

Popper, Karl (1976). 'A Note on Verisimilitude', *The British Journal for the Philosophy of Science*, Vol. 27, pp. 147–159.

Popper, Karl (1983). *Realism and the Aim of Science*, W. W. Bartley III (ed.), London: Hutchinson.

Popper, Karl (1985). "The Rationality Principle," in: David Miller (ed.) *Popper Selections*, Princeton: Princeton University Press.

Portmore, Douglas (2011). *Commonsense Consequentialism: Wherein Morality Meets Rationality*, New York: Oxford University Press.

Quine, Willard Van Orman (1976). *The Ways of Paradox*, Cambridge MA: Harvard University Press.

Quine, Willard Van Orman (1986). *The Philosophy of Logic*, Cambridge MA: Harvard University Press.

Quine, Willard Van Orman (1992). *Pursuit of Truth*, Cambridge MA: Harvard University Press.

Rauniyar, Ganesh and Kanbur, Ravi (2010). "Inclusive Development: Two papers on Conceptualization, Application and the ADB Perspective", *Journal of the Asia Pacific Economy*, Vol. 15, No. 4, pp. 437–469.

Razin, Assaf and Rosefielde, Steven (2012). "What Really Ails the Eurozone?: Faulty Supranational Architecture," *Contemporary Economics*, Vol. 6, No. 4, pp. 10–18.

Reinhart, Carmen and Rogoff, Kenneth (2009). *This Time Will be Different: Eight Centuries of Financial Folly*, Princeton, NJ: Princeton University Press.

Robinson, Joan (1962). *Economic Philosophy*, London: C.A. Watts.

Rosefielde, Steven (1981). "Knowledge and Socialism," in Rosefielde, ed., *Economic Welfare and the Economics of Soviet Socialism*, Cambridge UP, London, pp. 5–24.

Rosefielde, Steven (1988). "The Soviet Economy in Crisis: Birman's Cumulative Disequilibrium Hypothesis," *Soviet Studies*, Vol. XL, No. 1, pp. 222–244.

Rosefielde, Steven (2002). *Comparative Economic Systems: Culture, Wealth and Power in the 21st Century*, London: Blackwell.

Rosefielde, Steven (2003). "The Riddle of Postwar Soviet Economic Growth: Statistics Lied and Were Misconstrued," *Europe-Asia Studies*, Vol. 53, No. 3, pp. 469–481.

Rosefielde, Steven (2005). "Russia: An Abnormal Country," European *Journal of Comparative Economics*, Vol. 2, No. 1, pp. 3–16.

Rosefielde, Steven (June 2005). "Tea Leaves and Productivity: Bergsonian Norms for Gauging the Soviet Future," *Comparative Economic Studies*, Vol. 47, No. 2, pp. 259–273.

Rosefielde, Steven (2007). *Russian Economy from Lenin to Putin*, New York: Wiley.

Rosefielde, Steven (2010). *Red Holocaust*, New York: Routledge.

Rosefielde, Steven (2012). "The 'Impossibility of Russian Economic Reform: Waiting for Godot," in Stephen Blank (ed.), *Russian Reform*, Carlisle Barracks: US Army War College.

Rosefielde, Steven (2013). "Soviet Economy: An Ideocratic Reassessment," *Ekonomicheskaya Nauka Sovremennoy Rossii*, #3.

Rosefielde, Steven (2013). *Asian Economic Systems*, Singapore: World Scientific Publishers.

Rosefielde, Steven and Hedlund, Stefan (2008). *Russia Since 1980: Wrestling With Westernization*, Cambridge: Cambridge University Press.

Rosefielde, Steven, Kuboniwa, Masaaki and Mizobata, Satoshi (2012). *Prevention and Crisis Management: Lessons for Asia from the 2008 Crisis*, Singapore: World Scientific.

Rosefielde, Steven and Mills, Daniel Quinn (2013). *Democracy and Its Elected Enemies: American Political Capture and Economic Decline*, Cambridge: Cambridge University Press.

Rosefielde, Steven and Pfouts, Ralph W. (June 1986) "The Firm in Illyria: Market Syndicalism Revisited," *Journal of Comparative Economics*, Vol. 10, No. 2, pp. 160–170.

Rosefielde, Steven and Pfouts, Ralph W. (1995). "Economic Optimization and Technical Efficiency in Soviet Enterprises Jointly Regulated by Plans and Incentives," *European Economic Review*, Vol. 32, No. 6, pp. 1285–1299.

Rosenberg, Alex and Curtain, Tyler (2013). "What is Economics Good For?" *The Stone*.

Rosenberg, Alexander (1994). *Mathematic Politics or Science of Diminishing Returns*, Chicago: University of Chicago Press.

Ross, Stephen (1973). "The Economic Theory of Agency: The Principal's Problem," *American Economic Review*, Vol. 63, No. 2, pp. 134–139.

Rousseau, Jean-Jacques (1754). *Discourse on the Origin and Basis of Inequality Among Men (Discours sur l'origine et les fondements de l'inégalité parmi les hommes)*.

Rousseau, Jean-Jacques (1962). *The Social Contract*, Book I, Chapter 1.

Rubinstein, Ariel (1998). *Modeling Bounded Rationality*, Cambridge MA: MIT Press.

Russell, Bertrand (1900). *A Critical Exposition of the Philosophy of Leibniz*, London: George Allen & Unwin.

Samuelson, Paul (1939). "The Interaction Between the Multiplier Analysis and the Principle of Acceleration," *Review of Economic Statistics*, Vol. 21, No. 2, pp. 75–78.

Samuelson, Paul (1947). *Foundations of Economic Analysis*, Cambridge MA: Harvard University Press.

Samuelson, Paul (1966). "Optimal Compacts for Redistribution," in Samuelson, *Collected Scientific Papers*, Vol. 4, Chapter 257, Cambridge MA: MIT Press.

Samuelson, Paul (1990). "Gibbs in Economics," in Proceedings of the Gibbs Symposium (Providence, RI), pp. 255–267.

Sargent, Thomas (2012). "Nobel Lecture: United States Then, Europe Now," *Journal of Political Economy*, Vol. 120, No. 1, pp. 1–40.

Sartre, Jean-Paul (1993). *Being and Nothingness: An Essay in Phenomenological Ontology*, New York: Washington Square Press.

Schmitt, Carl (2004). *Legality and Legitimacy*, Durham NC: Duke University Press, 2004.

Schumpeter, Joseph (1942). *Capitalism, Socialism and Democracy*, New York: Harper and Rowe.

Selten, Reinhard (2002). "What is Bounded Rationality?" in *Bounded Rationality: The Adaptive Toolbox*, Gigerenzer, Gerd and Selten, Reinhard (eds.), Cambridge, MA: MIT Press.

Sen, Amartya (2010). *The Idea of Justice*, London: Penguin.

Sen, Amartya (1979). "Personal Utilities and Public Judgements: Or What's Wrong with Welfare Economics," *Economic Journal*, Vol. 89, No. 355, pp. 537–588.

Shiller, Robert (2000). *Irrational Exuberance*, Princeton NJ: Princeton University Press.

Shliefer, Andrei and Treisman, Daniel (2004). "Russia: A Normal Country," *Foreign Affairs*, Vol. 83, March/April, pp. 20–38.

Simon, Herbert (1955). "A Behavioral Model of Rational Choice," *Quarterly Journal of Economics*, Vol. 59, pp. 99–118.

Simon, Herbert (1957). *Models of Man: Social and Rational-Mathematical Essays on Rational Human Behavior in a Social Setting*, New York: John Wiley.

Simon, Herbert (1959). "Theories of Decision Making in Economic Behavioral Science," *American Economic Review*, Vol. 49, pp. 99–118.

Simon, Herbert (1982). *Models of Bounded Rationality*, Cambridge, MA: Harvard University Press.

Simon, Herbert (1990). "A Mechanism for Social Selection and Successful Altruism," *Science*, Vol. 250 (4988), pp. 1665–1668.

Simon, Herbert (1991). "Bounded Rationality and Organizational Learning," *Organization Science*, Vol. 2, No. 1, pp. 125–134.

Simon, Herbert (1992). "Introductory Comment" in M. Egidi and R. Marris (eds.), *Economics, Bounded Rationality and the Cognitive Revolution*, Aldershot: Ashgate.

Simon, Herbert with Egidi, M. Marris R. and Viale, R. (1992). *Economics, Bounded Rationality and the Cognitive Revolution*, Aldershot: Ashgate.

Sims, Christopher (2012). "Gaps in the Institutional Structure of the Euro Area," *Public Debt*, Monetary Policy and Financial Stability. http://www.princeton.edu/jrc/events_archive/repository/inaugural-conference/Sims_Paper_Gaps.pdf.

Smith, Adam (1759). *Theory of Moral Sentiments*, London.

Smith, Adam (1776). *Inquiry into the Nature and Causes of the Wealth of Nations*, London: W. Strahan and T. Cadell.

Sonnenschein, H. (1971). "Demand Theory without Transitive Preferences," in J.S. Chipman *et al.* (eds.), *Utility, Preference and Demand: A Minnesota Symposium*, New York: Harcourt Brace Jovanovich, pp. 215–223.

Stanley Jevons, William (1866). "A General Mathematical Theory of Political Economy," *Journal of the Royal Statistical Society*, XXIX.

Sternberg, Robert (1990). *Wisdom: Its Nature, Origins, and Development*, Cambridge: Cambridge University Press.

Stiglitz, Joseph (2002). *Globalization and its Discontents*, London: Penguin.

Stiglitz, K. O. (1954)."Intransitivity, Utility and the Aggregation of Preference Patterns," *Econometrica*, Vol. 22, pp. 1–13.

Suzumura, Kotaro, Arrow, Kenneth and Sen, Amartya (eds.) (2002). *Handbook of Social Choice and Welfare*, Vol. 1, Amsterdam: Elsevier.

Swift, Jonathan (1726). *Gulliver's Travels*.

Taleb, Nassim (2007). *The Black Swan: The Impact of the Highly Improbable*, New York: Random House.

Tisdell, Clem (1996). *Bounded Rationality and Economic Evolution: A Contribution to Decision Making, Economics, and Management*, Cheltenham, UK: Brookfield.

Tversky, A. (1969). "Intransitivity of Preferences," *Psychological Review*, Vol. 2, pp. 31–48.

Vanek, Jaroslav (1970). *The General Theory of Labor-Managed Market Economies*, Ithaca, NY: Cornell University Press.

Vogl, Joseph (2014). *The Specter of Capital*, Palo Alto: Stanford University Press.

Voltaire, Candide (1759). *ou l'Optimisme*.

Walras, Marie-Esprit-Leon (1874). *Éléments d'économie politique pure*.

Ward, Benjamin (1958). "The Firm in Illyria: Market Syndicalism," *American Economic Review*, Vol. 48, No. 4, September, pp. 566–589.

Weber, Max (1978). *Economy and Society*, Berkeley CA: University of California Press.

Weintraub, Roy (1979). *Microfoundations: The Compatibility of Microeconomics and Macroeconomics*, Cambridge: Cambridge University Press.

Weitzman, Martin (1970). "Iterative Multi-Level Planning with Production Targets," *Econometrica*, Vol. 38, pp. 50–65.

Weitzman, Martin (1974). "Prices versus Quantities." *Review of Economic Studies*, Vol. 4, pp. 477–491.

Weitzman, Martin (1986). *The Share Economy: Conquering Stagflation*, Cambridge MA: Harvard University Press.

Wiencek, Henry (2012). *Master of the Mountain: Thomas Jefferson and His Slaves*, New York: Farrar, Strauss & Giroux.

Xu, Kuan (2003). "How has the Literature on Gini's Index Evolved in the Past 80 Years?," *China Economic Quarterly*, Vol. 2, pp. 757–778.

Zafirovski, Milan (2011). *The Enlightenment and its Effect on Modern Society*, New York: Springer.

Zmora, Hillary (1990). *Monarchy, Aristocracy, and the State in Europe — 1300–1800*, New York: Routledge.

Postscript

Ralph William Pfouts died on May 19, 2014 at the age of 93, a few months after *Inclusive Economic Theory* was completed. He earned his B.A. degree from the University of Kansas in 1942 and served as commander of an American destroyer in the Japanese theater during World War II. He received his M.A. in 1947 and Ph.D. in economics from the University of North Carolina in 1952, whereupon he was immediately appointed as Associate Professor. Bill and Kenneth Arrow were Harold Hotelling's most famous students. Bill was promoted to the rank of Full Professor in 1958, retiring in 1987. He was both Vice President and President of the Southern Economic Association (1961–1962; 1965–1966) as well as the Atlantic Economic Society (1973–1976; 1977–1978) which bestowed a Lifetime Achievement Award on him in 2008. He also held responsible positions in the American Economic Association, the American Statistical Association, the Econometric Society, and the International Institute of Arts and Letter. Bill was a visiting scholar at the Social Science Research Council, Department of Applied Economics, Cambridge University (1953–1954) and the Massachusetts Institute of Technology (1962–1963) where he worked with Paul Samuelson on consumption theory and the theory of multiproduct firms. During the Gorbachev years, he and Steve Rosefielde collaborated with the Central Economics and Mathematics Institute (Moscow) investigating Soviet enterprise efficiency and transition possibilities. Bill's research was concentrated in mathematical microeconomics and statistics. He published widely in well-respected journals and always kept advancing the state of economic science. He collaborated with

Rosefielde and George Kleiner (Deputy Director of the Central Economics and Mathematics Institute, Moscow) on diverse aspects of comparative economic systems theory from the late 1970s onwards. Bill and Steve had shared interests in methodology, production function theory, egalitarianism and the theory of labor managed firms. They collaborated on these issues for a half century. Their joint articles included: "The Firm in Illyria: Market Syndicalism Revisited," *Journal of Comparative Economics*, Vol. 10, No. 2, June 1986, pp. 160–170; "Economic Optimization and Technical Efficiency in Soviet Enterprises Jointly Regulated by Plans and Incentives," *European Economic Review*, Vol. 32, No. 6, 1988, pp. 1285–1299; and "Neoclassical Norms and the Valuation of National Product in the Soviet Union and Its Postcommunist Successor States", *Journal of Comparative Economics*, Vol. 21, No. 3, December 1995, pp. 375–389. *Inclusive Economic Theory* is the capstone of their quest to construct a unified field theory of economic behavior.

Index

200   *Index*

Printed in the United States
By Bookmasters